A-Z

Street Atlas of
PRESTON

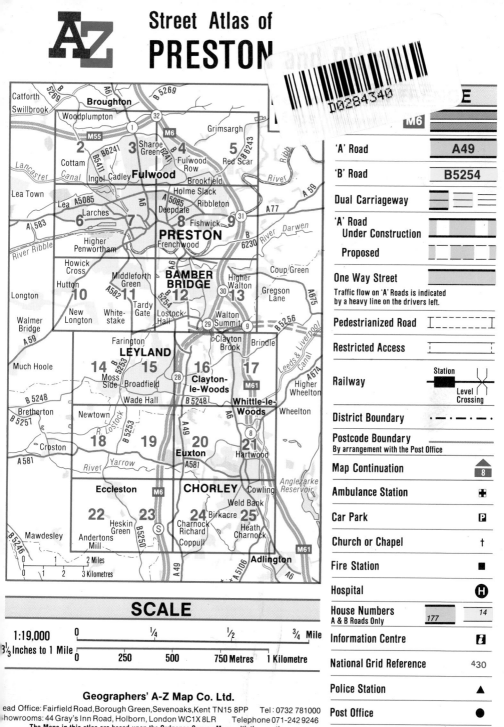

'A' Road	**A49**
'B' Road	**B5254**
Dual Carriageway	
'A' Road Under Construction	
Proposed	
One Way Street	

Traffic flow on 'A' Roads is indicated by a heavy line on the drivers left.

Pedestrianized Road	
Restricted Access	
Railway	Station / Level Crossing
District Boundary	—·—·—
Postcode Boundary By arrangement with the Post Office	
Map Continuation	▲ 8
Ambulance Station	✚
Car Park	P
Church or Chapel	†
Fire Station	■
Hospital	H
House Numbers A & B Roads Only	177 14
Information Centre	i
National Grid Reference	430
Police Station	▲
Post Office	●
Toilet	▽
with Disabled Facilities	♿

SCALE

1:19,000
3⅓ Inches to 1 Mile

0   ¼   ½   ¾ Mile

0   250   500   750 Metres   1 Kilometre

Geographers' A-Z Map Co. Ltd.

Head Office: Fairfield Road, Borough Green, Sevenoaks, Kent TN15 8PP   Tel : 0732 781000
Showrooms: 44 Gray's Inn Road, Holborn, London WC1X 8LR   Telephone 071-242 9246

The Maps in this atlas are based upon the Ordnance Survey Maps with the sanction of The Controller of Her Majesty's Stationery Office. Crown Copyright Reserved.

© 1992   Edition 2   Copyright of the Publishers

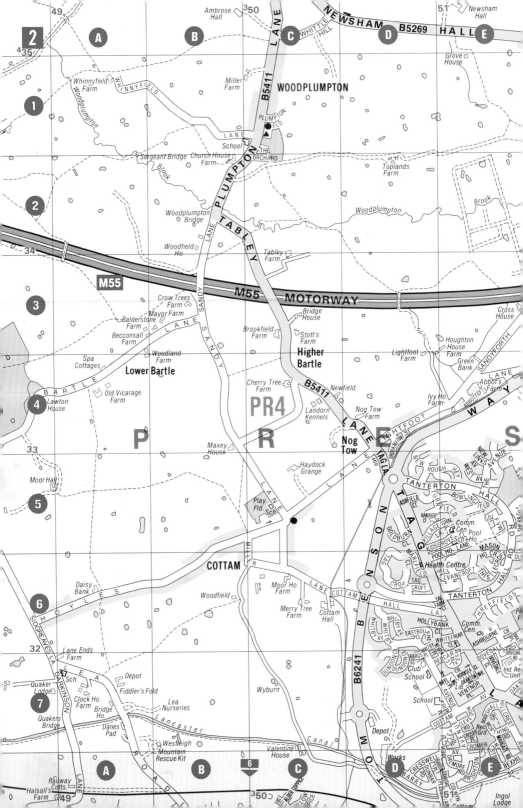

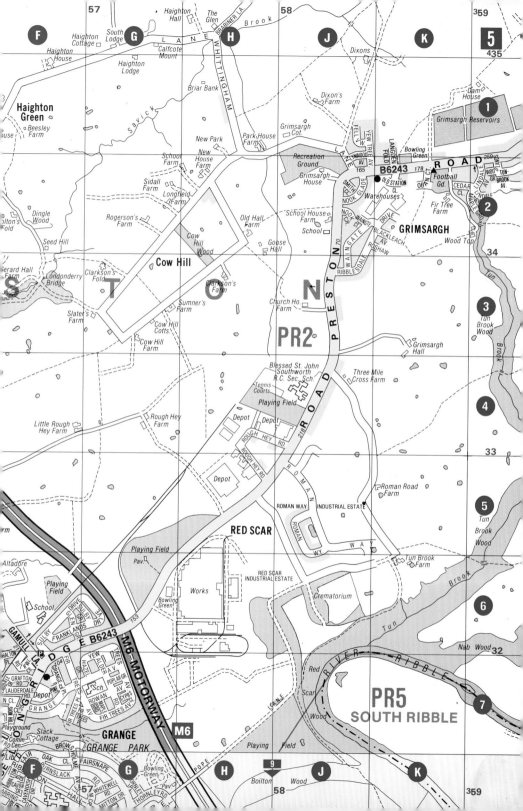

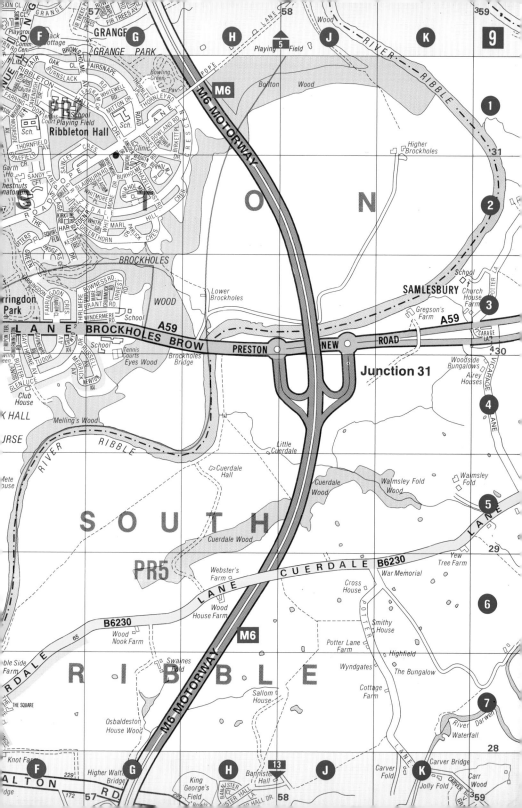

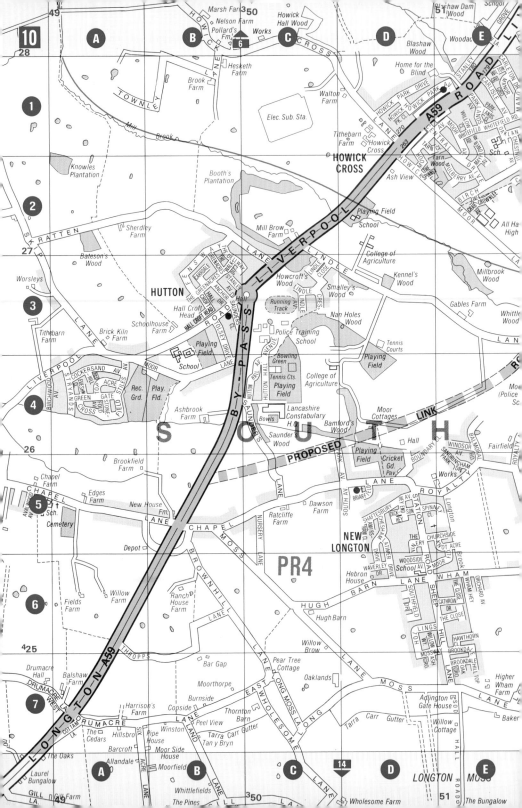

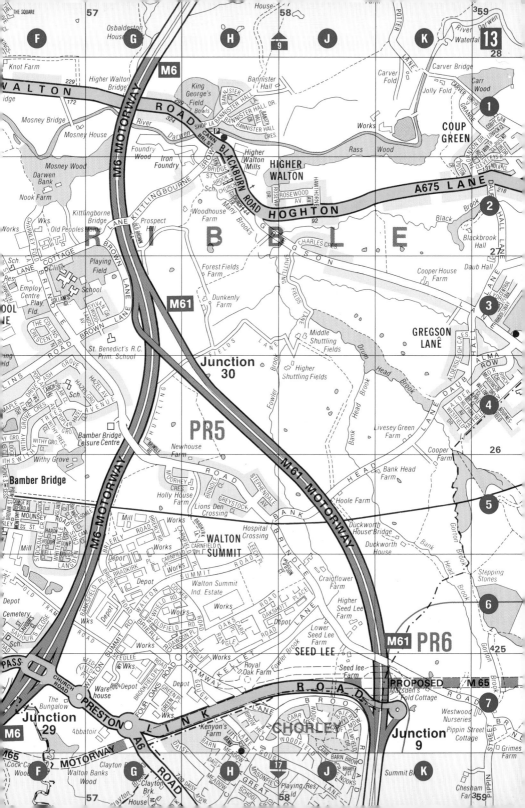

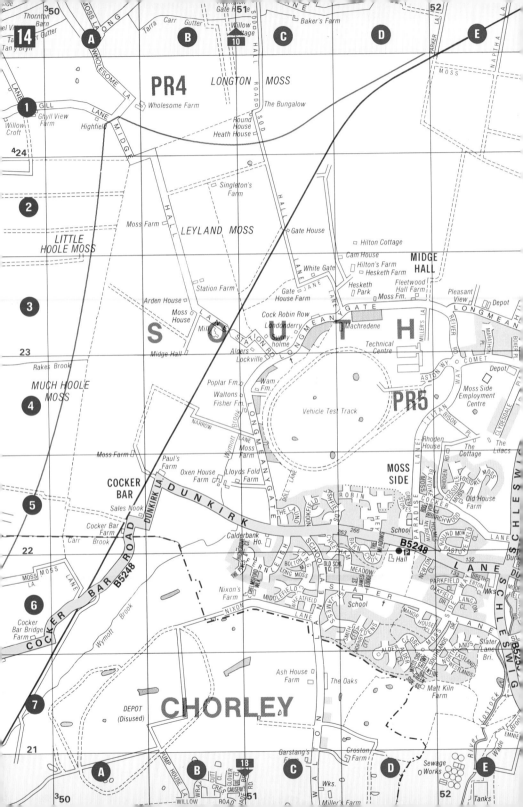

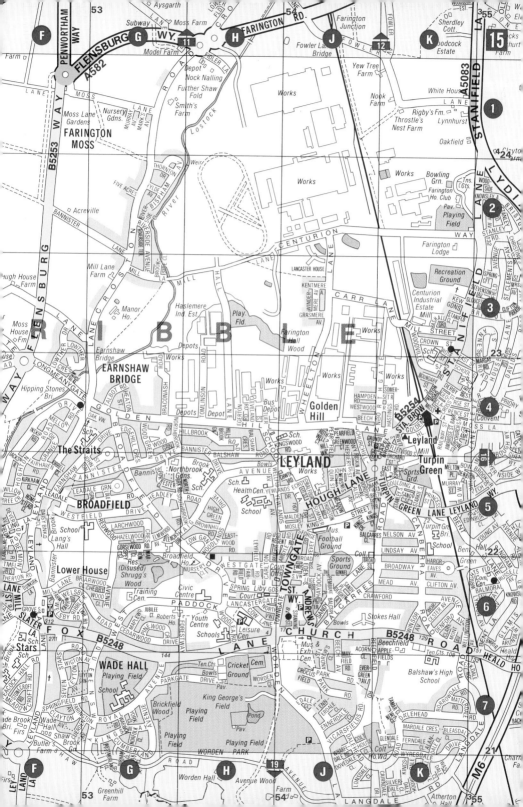

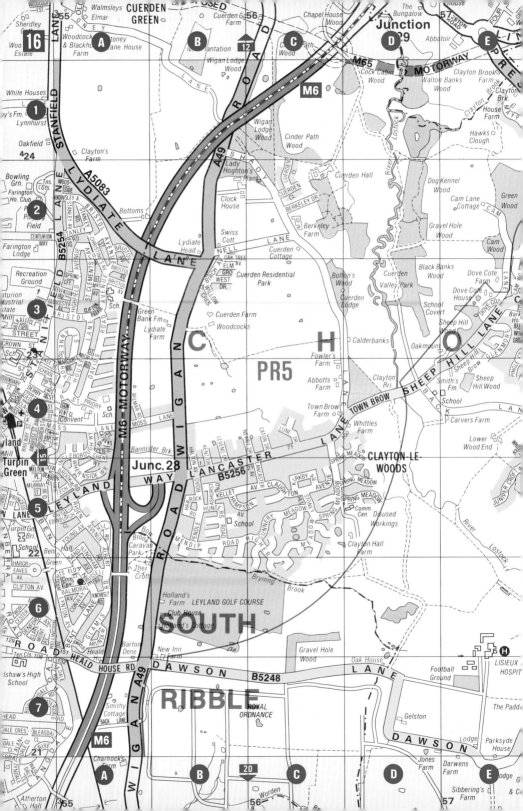

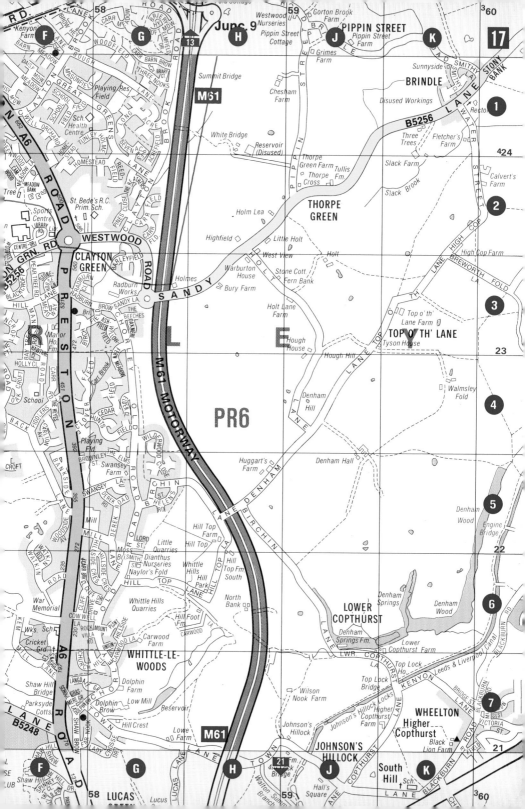

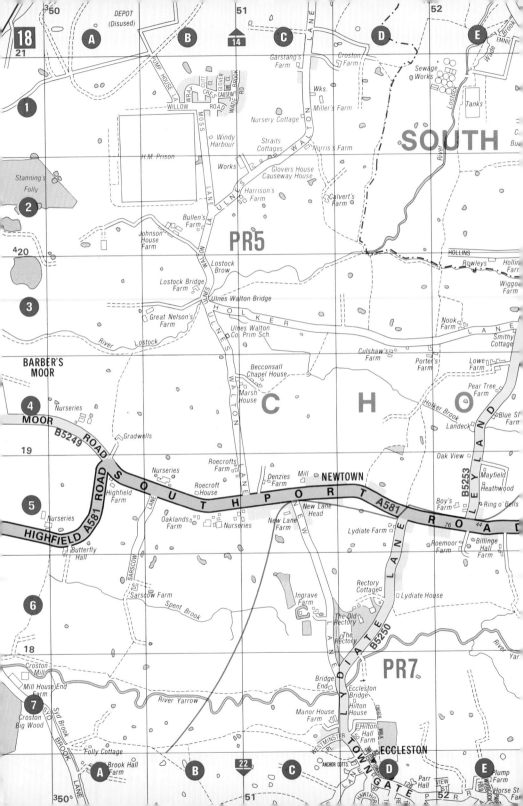

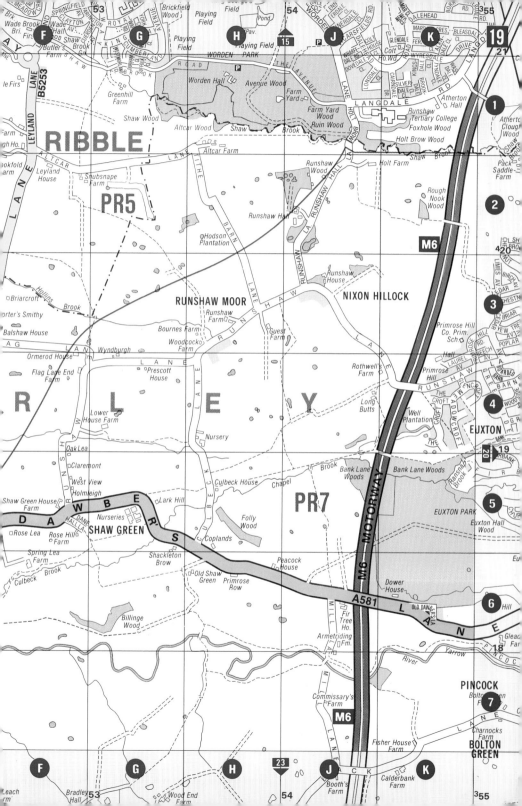

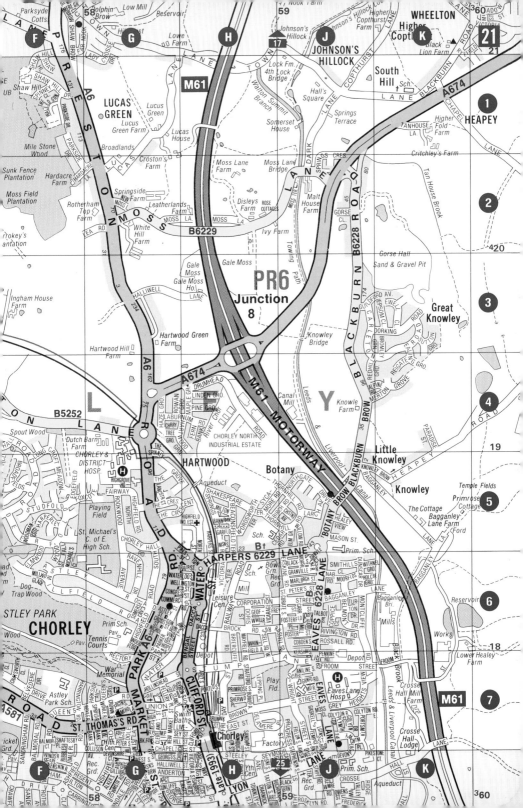

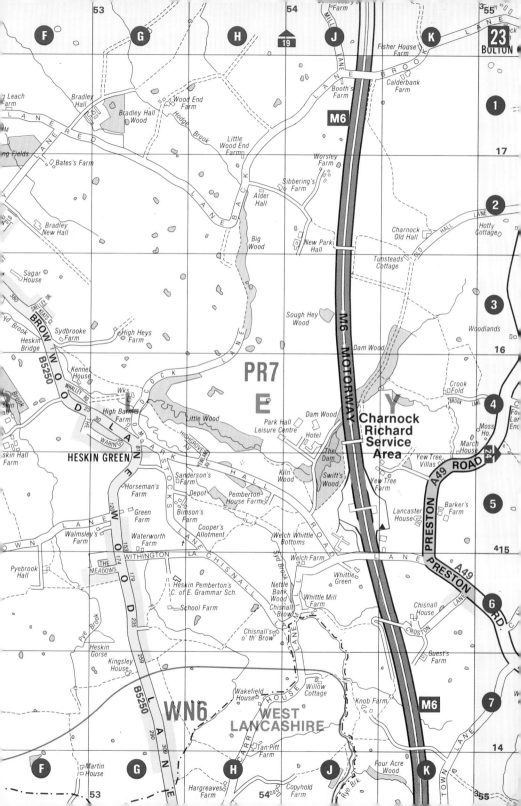

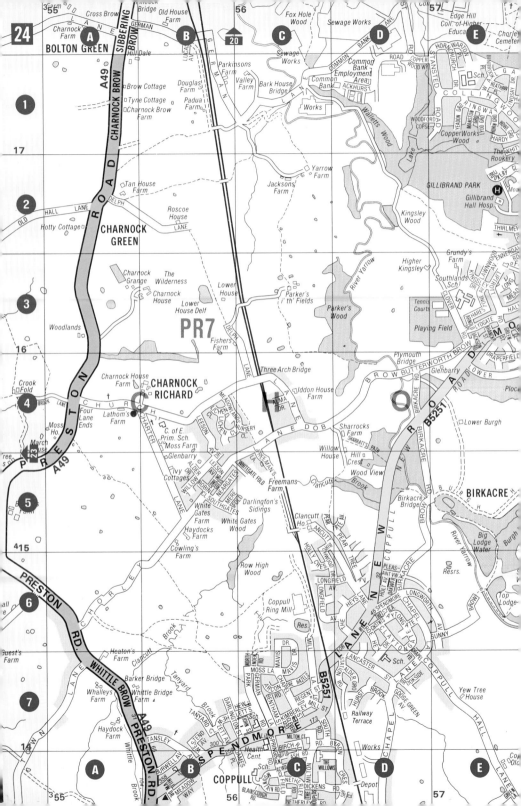

INDEX TO STREETS

HOW TO USE THIS INDEX

(a) A strict alphabetical order is followed in which Av., Rd., St., etc. are read in full and as part of the name preceding them; e.g. Abbotsway. follows Abbot Meadow. but precedes Abbott Croft.

(b) Each Street is followed by its Postal Code District Number and map reference; e.g. Abbey St. PR2—4H 7 is in the Preston 2 Postal Code District and is to be found in square 4H on page 7.

(c) Street and subsidiary names not shown on the Maps, appear in *Italics* with the thoroughfare to which it is connected shown in brackets.

N.B. The Postal Code District Numbers given in this index are, in fact, only the first part of the Postcode to each address and are only meant to indicate the Postal Code District in which each street is situated.

ABBREVIATIONS USED IN THIS INDEX

All : Alley
App : Approach
Arc : Arcade
Av : Avenue
Bk : Back
Boulevd : Boulevard
Bri : Bridge
B'way : Broadway
Bldgs : Buildings
Chyd : Churchyard
Cir : Circus
Clo : Close
Comn : Common
Ct : Court

Cres : Crescent
Dri : Drive
E : East
Embkmt : Embankment
Est : Estate
Gdns : Gardens
Ga : Gate
Gt : Great
Grn : Green
Gro : Grove
Ho : House
Ind : Industrial
Junct : Junction
La : Lane

Lit : Little
L : Liverpool
Lwr : Lower
Mans : Mansions
Mkt : Market
M : Mews
Mt : Mount
N : North
Pal : Palace
Pde : Parade
Pk : Park
Pas : Passage
Pl : Place
PR : Preston

Prom : Promenade
Rd : Road
S : South
Sq : Square
Sta : Station
St : Street
Ter : Terrace
Up : Upper
Vs : Villas
Wlk : Walk
W : West
WN : Wigan
Yd : Yard

Abbey St. PR2—4H 7
Abbey Wlk. PR1—3H 11
Abbot Meadow. PR1—1H 11
Abbotsway. PR1—6G 7
Abbott Croft. PR4—4E 2
Abingdon Dri. PR2—3E 6
Acacia Rd. PR2—2E 8
Ackhurst Rd. PR7—7D 20
Acorn Clo. PR5—6J 15
Acrefield. PR5—1G 17
Acregate La. PR1—3D 8
Acreswood Clo. PR7—7C 24
Adelaide St. PR1—4B 8
Adelphi Pl. PR1—4K 7
Adelphi St. PR1—3J 7
Agnes St. PR1—4A 8
Ainsdale Dri. PR2—2B 6
Ainslie Rd. PR2—1J 7
Alandale Clo. PR5—7K 15
Albany Dri. PR5—3D 12
Albatross St. PR1—3B 8
Albert Rd. PR1—2K 7
Albert Rd. PR2—1K 7
Albert Rd. PR5—5A 16
Albert St. PR7—1H 25
Albion St. PR7—1G 25
Albrighton Clo. PR5—6B 12
Albrighton Cres. PR5—6B 12
Albrighton Rd. PR5—6B 12
Albyn Bank Rd. PR1—5B 8
Albyn St. E. PR1—5B 8
Alcester Av. PR1—7G 7
Aldate Gro. PR2—2E 6
Aldcliffe Rd. PR2—3C 6
Alder Clo. PR5—6D 14
Alder Coppice. PR2—1C 6
Alder Dri. PR5—4K 13
Alder Dri. PR7—5B 24
Alderfield. PR1—2H 11
Alder Gro. PR7—7D 24
Alder Rd. PR2—7G 5
Aldersleigh Cres. PR5—4K 13
Aldfield Av. PR2—3A 6
Aldred St. PR6—1H 25
Aldwych Dri. PR2—2D 6
Aldwych Dri. PR5—6B 12
Alert St. PR2—3G 7
Alexandra Dri. PR5—2D 12
Alexandra St. PR1—5C 8
Alford Fold. PR2—4H 3

Alfred's Ct. PR7—1G 25
Alice Av. PR5—5J 15
Alker La. PR7—4E 20
Alker St. PR7—1G 25
Allenby Av. PR2—7B 4
Allengate. PR2—7K 3
Allerton Rd. PR5—2D 12
Alma Dri. PR4—7C 24
Alma Row. PR5—4K 13
Alma St. PR1—3A 8
Almond Clo. PR1—2F 11
Almond Clo. PR2—5D 4
Almond St. PR1—4B 8
Alpine Av. PR5—6B 12
Alpine Clo. PR5—6B 12
Alpine Rd. PR6—4J 21
Alsop St. PR1—2K 7
Alston St. PR1—3D 8
Altcar La. PR5—2F 19
Alvern Av. PR2—7H 3
Alvern Cres. PR2—7H 3
Ambleside Av. PR7—6B 20
Ambleside Clo. PR5—3E 12
Ambleside Rd. PR2—6E 4
Ambleside Wlk. PR2—6E 4
Ambrose St. PR5—4K 15
Amersham Clo. PR4—5D 10
Ampleforth Dri. PR5—4A 12
Anchor Cotts. PR7—1D 22
Anchor Ct. PR1—5K 7
Anchor Dri. PR4—3B 10
Anderton Rd. PR7—6B 20
Anderton St. PR7—1G 25
Andertons Way. PR2—6C 4
Andrew St. PR1—3C 8
Aniline St. PR6—7J 21
Annis St. PR1—4C 8
Ansdell Gro. PR2—1G 7
Ansdell St. PR1—3C 8
Appleby Clo. PR5—4K 13
Appleby St. PR1—3K 7
Applefields. PR5—7K 15
Appletree Clo. PR1—3G 11
Aqueduct St. PR1—3H 7
Archway Bldgs. PR2—3E 6
Arcon Rd. PR7—7C 24
Ardee Rd. PR1—6H 7
Argyle Rd. PR5—5J 15
Argyll Rd. PR1—3A 8
Arkwright Rd. PR2—2K 7

Arley St. PR7—7H 21
Armstrong St. PR2—2F 7
Arnhem Rd. PR1—4D 8
(in two parts)
Arnold Clo. PR2—2E 8
Arnold Pl. PR7—3E 24
Arno St. PR1—5B 8
Arnott Rd. PR2—2G 7
Arnside Rd. PR2—2C 6
Arnside Rd. PR3—1H 3
Arroyo Way. PR2—7B 4
Arthur St. PR1—5J 7
Arthur St. PR6—1H 25
Arundel Pl. PR1—5A 8
Arundel Way. PR5—6A 16
Ashbourne Cres. PR2—6E 2
Ashby St. PR7—2G & 2H 25
Ash Coppice. PR2—2B 6
Asheldon St. PR1—3D 8
Ashfield. PR2—3K 3
Ashfield. PR6—3G 17
Ashfield Ct. PR5—5D 2
Ashfield Rd. PR7—1F 25
Ashfields. PR5—5C 14
Ashford Cres. PR3—1G 3
Ashford Rd. PR2—2C 6
Ash Gro. PR4—7D 10
Ash Gro. PR1—3E 8
Ash Gro. PR5—4F 13
Ash Gro. PR7—3G 25
Ashleigh Ct. PR2—4A 4
Ashleigh St. PR1—5C 8
Ash Meadow. PR2—1B 6
Ashmoor St. PR1—3J 7
Ashness Clo. PR2—3K 3
Ash Rd. PR7—7C 24
Ashton Clo. PR2—3E 6
Ashton St. PR2—4H 7
Ashtree Ct. PR2—7E 2
Ashtree Gro. PR1—1F 11
Ashurst Rd. PR5—5B 16
Ashworth Gro. PR1—6C 8
Ashworth La. PR1—6B 8
Ashworth St. PR1—5B 8
Ashworth St. PR5—3F 13
Asland Clo. PR5—5F 13
Aspden St. PR1—4C 8
Aspden St. PR5—4E 12
Aspels Cres. PR1—1G 11

Aspels Nook. PR1—1G 11
Aspels, The. PR1—1G 11
Aspinall Clo. PR1—3H 11
Asshawes, The. PR6—7K 25
Assheton Pl. PR2—1E 8
Astley Rd. PR7—6F 21
Astley St. PR7—6G 21
Aston Way. PR5—4D 14
Athelstan Fold. PR2—1G 7
Atherton Rd. PR5—6F 15
Athol Gro. PR6—2J 25
Atholl St. PR1—4H 7
Aubigny Dri. PR2—7H 3
Aughton Wlk. PR1—3K 7
Austin Cres. PR2—7F 3
Avalwood Av. PR4—5A 10
Avenham Colonnade. PR1 —6A 8
Avenham Ct. PR1—5A 8
Avenham La. PR1—6A 8
Avenham Pl. PR1—6A 8
Avenham Rd. PR1—5A 8
Avenham Rd. PR7—1G 25
Avenham St. PR1—5A 8
Avenham Ter. PR1—6A 8
Avenham Wlk. PR1—6A 8
Avenue, The. PR1—7F 7
Avenue, The. PR2—5E 2
(Ingol)
Avenue, The. PR2—3B 6
(Lea)
Avenue, The. PR5—1H 19
Avenue, The. PR6—7K 25
Avon Bri. PR2—3G 3
Avondale Dri. PR5—5B 12
Avondale Rd. PR2—1G 25
Aysgarth Av. PR2—4K 3
Azalea Clo. PR2—5C 4

Bk. Club St. PR5—6E 12
Bk. Fazakerley St. PR7—7G 21
Bk. Grimshaw St. PR1—5A 8
Back La. L40—7A 22
Back La. PR6—4D 16
Back La. PR7—2H 23 to 7A 20
(Charnock Richard)
Back La. PR7—7A 16
(Leyland)
Back La. E. L40—7A 22

Bk. Seed St. PR1—4K 7
Bk. Starkie St. PR1—6K 7
Badgers Croft. PR2—2F 9
Badgers Way. PR5—2B 12
Bagganley La. PR6—5J & 6J 21
Bagnold Rd. PR1—3D 8
Bairstow St. PR1—5K 7
Baker St. PR5—4K 15
Balcarres Clo. PR5—5J 15
Balcarres Pl. PR5—6J 15
Balcarres Rd. PR2—2G 7
Balcarres Rd. PR5—6J 15
Balcarres Rd. PR7—3F 25
Balderstone Rd. PR1—7H 7
Baldwin. PR5—4E 12
Balfour Rd. PR2—1J 7
Balfour St. PR5—5J 15
Ballam Rd. PR2—3C 6
Balmoral Av. PR5—6A 16
Balmoral Ct. PR7—7F 21
Balmoral Rd. PR4—4E 10
Balmoral Rd. PR5—2D 12
Balmoral Rd. PR7—7F 21
(Chorley)
Balmoral Rd. PR7—1E 22
(Eccleston)
Balniel Clo. PR7—1F 25
Balshaw Av. PR7—5B 20
Balshaw Cres. PR5—4H 15
Balshaw La. PR7—6B 20
Balshaw Rd. PR5—4H 15
Bamber St. PR7—3F 25
Bamber's Yd. PR1—5K 7
Banastre. PR7—5E 20
Banbury Dri. PR2—7J 3
Bank Head La. PR5—5J 13
Bank La. PR7—4A 20
Bank Pde. PR1—2H 11
(Penwortham)
Bank Pde. PR1—6A 8
(Preston)
Bank Pl. PR2—3G 7
Banksfield Av. PR2—1G 7
Banksfield Pl. PR5—6G 13
Bankside. PR6—5F 17
Banks Rd. PR2—1G 7
Bank St. PR7—7G 21
Banner Clo. PR7—1D 22
Bannerman Ter. PR6—5H 21
Bannister Clo. PR5—1H 13
Bannister Dri. PR5—5F 15
Bannister Grn. PR7—6D 22
Bannister Hall Cres. PR5
—1H 13
Bannister Hall Dri. PR5—1H 13
Bannister Hall La. PR5—1H 13
Bannister La. PR5—2F 15
Bannister La. PR7—3E 22
Bannisters Bit. PR1—3G 11
Bannister St. PR7—1G 25
Barden Pl. PR2—7D 4
Bardsea Pl. PR2—1D 6
Barley Field. PR5—3G 17
Barlow St. PR1—2J to 2K 7
(in three parts)
Barmskin La. PR7—7D 22
Barnacre Clo. PR2—3A 4
Barn Croft. PR1—7F 7
Barn Croft. PR5—5D 14
Barnfield. PR5—5A 12
Barn Meadow. PR5—7H 13
Barnsfold. PR2—5H 3
Barnside. PR7—4A 20
Barons Way. PR7—5B 20
Barry Av. PR2—1G 9
Bartle La. PR4—4A 2
Bartle Pl. PR2—3C 6
Bashall Gro. PR3—3K 15
Bashaw St. PR5—3E 12
Basil St. PR1—2C 8
Bath St. PR2—3H 7
Bay Rd. PR2—2E 8
Baytree Clo. PR5—5C 12
Bay Tree Rd. PR6—4F 17
Beachley Rd. PR2—7E 2

Beacon Av. PR2—6H 3
Beaconfield Av. PR1—3F 9
Beacon Gro. PR2—7H 3
Beaconsfield Ter. PR6—5H 21
Beacon St. PR7—1H 25
Beatty Av. PR7—2F 25
Beaumaris Rd. PR5—6A 16
Beckett Ct. PR1—3K 7
Bedford Rd. PR2—7A 4
Bedford St. PR7—2G 25
Beech Av. PR5—6J 15
Beech Av. PR7—3A 20
Beeches, The. PR2—3H 3
Beeches, The. PR6—3G 17
Beechfield Rd. PR5—6K 15
Beechfields, The. PR7—2D 22
Beech Gro. PR2—3F 7
Beech Rd. PR5—4J 15
Beech St. PR1—6H 7
Beech St. S. PR1—6J 7
Beech Ter. PR1—6J 7
Beechway. PR1—1F 11
Beechway. PR2—7A 4
Beechwood Av. PR2—7G 3
Beechwood Av. PR5—1C 12
Beechwood Croft. PR6—3E 16
Beechwood Rd. PR7—2J 25
Bee La. PR1—4H 11
Beenland St. PR1—3D 8
Belgrave Av. PR1—2F 11
Belgrave Rd. PR5—6H 15
Belmont Av. PR2—2D 8
Belmont Clo. PR2—2D 8
Belmont Cres. PR2—2D 8
Belmont Dri. PR6—6J 21
Belmont Rd. PR2—2G 7
Belmont Rd. PR5—2F 15
Belton Hill. PR2—3H 3
Belvedere Dri. PR7—7F 21
Belvedere Rd. PR5—4K 15
Bence Rd. PR1—5B 8
Bengal St. PR7—7H 21
(in two parts)
Bentham St. PR7—7C 24
Bent La. PR5—5K 15
Bentley La. L40 & PR7—7B 22
Benton Rd. PR2—7D 4
Berkeley Dri. PR7—3H 25
Berkeley Dri. PR5—2C 16
Berkeley St. PR1—3J 7
Berry Field. PR1—2G 11
Berry St. PR1—5A 8
Berry St. PR5—5A 12
Berwick Dri. PR2—7H 3
Berwick Rd. PR1—5A 8
Berwick St. PR1—3E 8
Beverley Clo. PR2—4G 7
Bexhill Rd. PR2—1E 6
Bidstone St. PR1—4E 8
Bilsborough Hey. PR1—4J 11
Bilsborough Meadow. PR2
—1C 6
Binbrook Pl. PR7—1E 24
Birch Av. PR1—2E 10
Birch Av. PR2—2E 6
Birch Av. PR5—3B 16
Birch Av. PR7—3A 20
Birch Cres. PR4—4K 13
Birchover Clo. PR2—6E 2
Birch Rd. PR6—5H 21
Birch Rd. PR7—7C 24
Birchwood PR5—5E 14
Birchwood Av. PR4—4A 10
Birchwood Dri. PR2—4H 3
Birchwood Dri. PR7—6C 24
Bird St. PR1—6H 7
Birkacre Brow. PR7—6D 24
Birkacre Rd. PR7—4D 24
(in two parts)
Birkdale Dri. PR2—2C 6
Birkett Dri. PR2—1G 9
Birkett Pl. PR2—1G 9
Birk St. PR1—5J 7

Birley St. PR1—4K 7
Birtwistle St. PR5—6B 12
Bishopgate. PR1—4A 8
Bishopsway. PR1—2H 11
Bison Pl. PR5—4E 14
Bispham Av. PR5—2G 15
Bispham St. PR1—4K 7
Blackberry Way. PR1—3G 11
Black Bull La. PR2—6H 3
Blackburn Brow. PR6—5J 21
Blackburn Rd. PR5—1H 13
Blackburn Rd. PR6
(in two parts)—3J 21 to 6K 17
Blackburn St. PR6—1J 25
Blackcroft. PR6—3F 17
Black Horse St. PR7—2F 25
Blackleach Av. PR2—2K 5
Blackpool Rd. PR2 & PR1
—3A 6 to 3E 8
Blackstone St. PR1—6J 21
Blackthorn Clo. PR2—3B 6
Blackthorn Croft. PR6—4E 16
Blackthorn Dri. PR1—2F 11
Blainscough Rd. PR7—7C 24
Blake Av. PR5—6A 12
Blanche St. PR2—3G 7
Blashaw La. PR1—7E 6
Blaydike Moss. PR5—5D 14
Bleachers Dri. PR5—5G 15
Bleasdale Clo. PR5—5F 13
(Bamber Bridge)
Bleasdale Clo. PR5—7K 15
(Leyland)
Bleasdale St. E. PR1—3B 8
Blelock St. PR1—5A 8
Blenheim Clo. PR5—5C 12
Bloomfield Ct. PR1—2J 7
Bloomfield Grange. PR1—3G 11
Blossoms, The. PR2—5C 4
Blue Bell Pl. PR1—4A 8
Blue Stone La. L40—5A 22
Blundell La. PR1—6F 7
Blundell Rd. PR2—1J 7
Boarded Barn. PR7—4A 20
Bodmin St. PR1—3D 8
Boegrave Av. PR5—5A 12
Bold St. PR1—2H 7
Bolton M. PR5—6C 14
Bolton Rd. PR7—2H 25
Bolton's Ct. PR1—5A 8
Bolton St. PR7—1G 25
Bone Croft. PR6—3F 17
Bootle St. PR1—3C 8
Borrowdale Rd. PR5—7K 15
Bostock St. PR1—5A 8
Botany Brow. PR6—5J 21
Boulevard. PR1—7B 8
Boundary Clo. PR4—5D 10
Boundary Rd. PR2—1H 7
Boundary St. PR5—4K 15
Bournesfield. PR2—3E 8
Bouverie St. PR1—3E 8
Bow Brook Rd. PR5—5K 15
Bowers Clo. PR5—5C 4
Bowland Av. PR6—7H 21
Bowland Pl. PR2—1H 5
Bowland Rd. PR2—1G 9
Bow La. PR1—5J 7
Bow La. PR5—5K 15
Bowlingfield. PR2—5E 2
Bowness Rd. PR1—3G 9
Bowran St. PR1—4J 7
Bow St. PR5—4K 15
Boxer Pl. PR5—3E 14
Boys La. PR2—6G 3
Brabiner La. PR2—1H 5
Bracewell Rd. PR2—6E 4
Brackenbury Clo. PR5—6A 12
Brackenbury Rd. PR2 & PR1
—1J 7
Brackenbury St. PR1
—2J & 2K 7
Braconash Rd. PR5—4G 15
Braddon St. PR1—3D 8
Bradkirk La. PR5—5H 13

Bradkirk Pl. PR5—6G 13
Bradley La. PR7—2E 22
Bradshaw La. L40—6A 22
Bradshaw La. PR6—7K 25
Bradshaws Brow. L40—7A 22
Braefield Cres. PR2—2F 9
Braintree Av. PR1—4J 11
Bramble Ct. PR1—3J 11
Brampton St. PR2—3G 7
Brancker St. PR7—3E 24
Brandiforth St. PR5—3F 13
Brant Rd. PR1—3G 9
Brayshaw Pl. PR2—7E 4
Bray St. PR2—3G 7
Bredon Av. PR7—6C 20
(in two parts)
Bredon Clo. PR7—6C 20
Breeze Mt. PR5—5C 12
Brennand Clo. PR5—5F 13
Bretherton Clo. PR5—6E 14
Bretherton Ter. PR5—5K 15
Breworth Fold La. PR6—3K 17
Briar Av. PR7—3A 20
Briarfield. PR4—5D 10
Briar Gro. PR2—7E 2
Briarwood Clo. PR5—6G 15
Briary Ct. PR5—1G 17
Bridge Bank. PR5—6C 8
Bridge Clo. PR5—5A 12
Bridge Ct. PR5—5A 12
Bridge End. PR5—5C 12
Bridge Rd. PR2—2G 7
Bridge Rd. PR5—5D 10
Bridge St. PR5—6E 12
(Bamber Bridge)
Bridge St. PR5—2H 13
(Higher Walton)
Bridge St. PR6—7K 17
Bridge Ter. PR5—6C 8
Bridgeway. PR5—5C 12
Briercliffe Rd. PR6—6H 21
Brierley Rd. PR5—6G 13
Brierley St. PR2—3H 7
Briers, The. PR7—2E 22
Briery Clo. PR7—7C 4
Brieryfield Rd. PR1—4H 7
Briery Hey. PR5—7J 13
Briggs Rd. PR2—2G 7
Brighton Cres. PR2—1E 6
Brighton St. PR6—7J 21
Brindle Clo. PR5—5H 13
Brindle Rd. PR5 & PR6
—3F 13 to 1K 17
Brindle St. PR1—4C 8
Brindle St. PR7—2G 25
Bristol Av. PR5—3A 16
Bristow Av. PR2—2F 7
Brixey St. PR1—6H 7
Brixton Rd. PR1—5B 8
Broadfield. PR3—1F 3
Broadfield Dri. PR1—3H 11
Broadfield Dri. PR5—4G 15
Broadfields. PR7—5F 21
Broadgate. PR1—6H 7
Broad Meadow. PR5—5A 12
Broad Oak Grn. PR1—2F 11
Broad Oak La. PR1—1F 11
Broad Sq. PR6—6J 15
Broad St. PR5—6J 15
Broadway. PR2—2D 6
(Ashton-on-Ribble)
Broadway. PR2—4H 3
(Fulwood)
Broadway. PR5—6K 15
Broadwood Clo. PR1—1F 11
Broadwood Dri. PR2—4J 3
Brockholes Brow. PR1 & PR2
—3G 9
Brockholes View. PR1—5C 8
Brock Rd. PR6—6H 21
Bromley Grn. PR6—3K 21
Bromley St. PR1—4H 7
Brook Croft. PR2—7F 3
Brookdale. PR4—7E 10
Brookdale Clo. PR5—1K 19

Brooke St. PR7 & PR6—1H 25
Brookfield Av. PR2—7C 4
Brookfield Dri. PR2—3J 3
Brookfield Pl. PR5—7G 13
Brookfield St. PR1—3K 7
Brookhouse St. PR2—3H 7
Brooklands. PR2—3E 6
Brooklands Av. PR2—4J 3
Brook La. PR4—6H 11
(in two parts)
Brook La. PR7—4K 23
Brookmeadow. PR4—4D 2
Brook Pl. PR2—2B 6
Brookside. PR7—7D 24
(Coppull)
Brookside. PR7—5A 20
(Euxton)
Brookside Clo. PR5—3G 15
Brookside Rd. PR2—4H 3
Brook St. PR2 & PR1
　　　　　—1H to 3J 7
Brook St. PR5—2H 13
Brook St. N. PR2—1H 7
Broomfield Mill St. PR1—3K 7
Broughton St. PR1—1J 7
Brow Hey. PR5—7H 13
Brownedge Clo. PR5—4D 12
Brownedge La. PR5—4D 12
Brownedge Rd. PR5—5A 12
Brownhill La. PR4—6B 10
Brownhill Rd. PR5—5H 15
Browning Cres. PR1—2D 8
Browning Rd. PR1—2D 8
Brown La. PR5—3G 13
Brownley St. PR6—1J 25
(Chorley)
Brownley St. PR6—5F 17
(Clayton-le-Woods)
Browns Hey. PR7—5E 20
Brown St. PR5—5F 13
Brown St. PR6—7H 21
Browsholme Av. PR2—7F 5
Brunswick Pl. PR2—3G 7
Brunswick St. PR6—7H 21
Brydeck Av. PR1—1J 11
Buchanan St. PR6—1H 25
Buckingham Av. PR1—3H 11
Buckingham St. PR6—1H 25
Bucklands Av. PR2—2H 7
Buckshaw Hall Clo. PR7—5F 21
Buller Av. PR1—1J 11
Bullfinch St. PR1—3B 8
Bullnose Rd. PR2—5E 6
Bulmer St. PR2—2G 7
Burgh Hall Rd. PR7—5E 24
Burgh La. PR7—6F & 4G 25
(in two parts)
Burgh Meadows. PR7—4G 25
Burholme Clo. PR2—2G 9
Burholme Pl. PR2—2G 9
Burholme Rd. PR2—2G 9
Burleigh Rd. PR1—5H 7
Burlington St. PR7—1H 25
Burnsall Pl. PR2—7E 4
Burnside Av. PR2—1F 9
Burnside Way. PR1—2H 11
Burnslack Rd. PR2—1F 9
Burns St. PR1—2D 8
Burrington Clo. PR2—5D 4
Burrow Rd. PR1—3A 8
Burwell Av. PR7—7B 24
Burwood Clo. PR1—4K 11
Burwood Dri. PR2—1E 8
Bushell Pl. PR1—6A 8
Bushell St. PR1—3K 7
Bussel Rd. PR1—3J 11
Butcher Brow. PR5—7E 8
Butler Pl. PR1—2K 7
Butlers Ct. PR1—5K 7
Butler St. PR1—5K 7
Butterlands. PR1—4F 9
Buttermere Av. PR7—2E 24
Buttermere Clo. PR2—7C 4
Buttermere Clo. PR5—3D 12
Butterworth Brow. PR7—4D 24

Bymbrig Clo. PR5—5E 12
Byron Cres. PR7—7D 24
Byron St. PR7—7H 21

Cadley Av. PR2—1F 7
Cadley Causeway. PR2—1G 7
Cadley Dri. PR2—1F 7
Cadogan Pl. PR1—6A 8
Cage La. PR4—5F 11
Cairndale Dri. PR5—1K 19
Cairnsmore Av. PR1—3F 9
Calder Av. PR2—5K 3
Calder Av. PR7—3F 25
Calder St. PR2—4F 7
Callon St. PR1—4D 8
Calverley St. PR1—3D 8
Cambridge Clo. PR1—2J 7
Cambridge Ct. PR1—2J 7
Cambridge Rd. PR5—5F 13
Cambridge Rd. PR1—2J 7
Cambridge St. PR7—1H 25
Cambridge Wlk. PR1—2J 7
Cam Clo. PR5—5F 13
Camden Pl. PR1—5K 7
Cam La. PR5—2E 16
Campbell St. PR1—4B 8
Cam St. PR1—2C 8
Camwood. PR5—2F 17
Camwood Dri. PR5—4B 12
Cam Wood Fold. PR6—3E 16
Canberra Rd. PR5—5K 15
Cann Bri. St. PR5—1H 13
Cannon Hill. PR2—3G 7
Cannon St. PR1—5K 7
Canterbury St. PR6—2J 25
Cantsfield Av. PR2—7F 3
Canute St. PR1—3A 8
Capitol Way. PR5—7C 8
Cardigan St. PR2—3H 7
Carleton Dri. PR1—1E 10
Carleton Rd. PR6—3J 21
Carlisle Av. PR1—1E 10
Carlisle St. PR1—4A 8
Carloway Clo. PR2—6C 4
Carlton Av. PR6—4F 17
Carlton Dri. PR1—7B 8
Carlton Rd. PR5—6H 15
Carlton St. PR2—4H 7
Carnarvon Rd. PR1—5H 7
Carnfield Pl. PR5—5H 13
Carnoustie Clo. PR2—4F 3
Carnoustie Ct. PR1—6E 6
Caroline St. PR1—4C 8
Carr Barn Brow. PR5—1G 17
Carr Brook Clo. PR6—6F 17
Carrdale. PR4—3B 10
Carr Field. PR5—2G 17
Carr Ho. La. WN6 & PR7—7H 23
Carrington Rd. PR7—1F 25
Carr La. PR5—3J 15
Carr La. PR7—3G 25
Carr Meadow. PR5—7J 13
Carrol St. PR1—3B 8
Carr Pl. PR5—6H 13
Carr Rd. PR6—4F 17
Carr St. PR1—5B 8
Carr St. PR5—5E 12
Carr St. PR6—6J 21
Carrwood Rd. PR1—2B 12
Carrwood Way. PR5—2B 12
Carter St. PR1—5H 7
Cartmel Pl. PR2—2C 6
(in two parts)
Cartmel Rd. PR5—6F 15
Carver Brow. PR5—1K 13
Carwood La. PR6—7G 17
Casterton. PR7—5A 20
Castle Clo. PR3—1K 11
Castle Mt. PR2—4K 3
Castle St. PR1—3K 7
Castle St. PR7—1H 25
Castleton Rd. PR1—3B 8
Castle Wlk. PR1—6G 7

Catforth Rd. PR2—3C 6
Catherine St. PR1—4B 8
Catherine St. PR7—2G 25
Cathrow Dri. PR4—6E 10
Caton Dri. PR5—4C 16
Causeway Av. PR2—7F 3
Causeway, The. PR5—1B 18
Cavendish Cres. PR2—1F 9
Cavendish Dri. PR2—1F 9
Cavendish Pl. PR5—2D 12
Cavendish Rd. PR1—3E 8
Cavendish St. PR6—1J 25
Cave St. PR1—4D 8
Caxton Rd. PR2—3B 4
Cecilia St. PR1—3D 8
Cedar Av. PR2—2E 6
Cedar Av. PR5—5B 12
Cedar Av. PR2—3A 20
Cedar Clo. PR2—2K 5
Cedar Field. PR6—4G 17
Cedar Rd. PR2—2E 8
Cedar Rd. PR6—5H 21
Cedars, The. PR7—4F 25
(Chorley)
Cedars, The. PR7—1D 22
(Eccleston)
Cedar Way. PR1—2F 11
Cedarwood Dri. PR5—6G 15
Cemetery Rd. PR1—3C 8
Central Av. PR5—3K 13
Central Dri. PR1—1D 10
Central Ter. PR7—3B 20
Centre Dri. PR6—2F 17
Centurion Way. PR5—2J 15
Chaddock St. PR1—5K 7
Chain Caul Rd. PR2—5C 6
Chain Caul Way. PR2—4C 6
Chain Ho. La. PR4—6G 11
Chalfont Field. PR2—6G 3
Chancery Rd. PR1—6D to 4E 20
Chandler St. PR1—4J 7
Channel Way. PR2—4G 7
Chapel Brow. PR5—4K 15
Chapel La. PR4—5A 10
Chapel La. PR6—1K 21
Chapel La. PR7—7D 24
Chapel Rd. PR2—7A 4
Chapel St. PR1—5K 7
Chapel St. PR7—7G 21
(Chorley)
Chapel St. PR7—7C 24
(Coppull)
Chapel Walks. PR1—5K 7
Chapel Yd. PR5—7D 8
Chapel Yd. PR7—7D 24
Chapman Rd. PR2—1A 8
Charles Cres. PR5—2J 13
Charleston Ct. PR5—4E 12
Charles Way. PR2—2C 6
Charlesway Ct. PR2—2C 6
Charlotte St. PR1—5A 8
Charnley Clo. PR1—3G 11
Charnley Fold La. PR5—2F 13
Charnley St. PR1—5A 8
Charnock Av. PR1—3J 11
Charnock Brow. PR7—1A 24
Charnock Fold. PR1—2A 8
Charnock St. PR1—2A 8
Charnock St. PR5—5J 15
Charnock St. PR6—1H 25
Charter La. PR7—4B 24
Chartwell Rise. PR5—5C 12
Chatburn Rd. PR2—7F 5
Chatham Pl. PR1—2B 8
Chatham Pl. PR6—7J 21
Chatsworth Clo. PR7—7F 21
Chatsworth Rd. PR5—5J 15
(Leyland)
Chatsworth Rd. PR5—2D 12
(Walton-le-Dale)
Chatsworth St. PR1—4C 8
Chaucer St. PR1—2D 8
Cheam Av. PR7—2H 25
Cheapside. PR1—5K 7
Cheapside. PR7—1G 25

Cheddar Dri. PR2—5D 4
Cheetham Meadow. PR5
　　　　　—5C 14
Chelford Clo. PR1—4K 11
Chelmsford Gro. PR7—1F 25
Chelmsford Pl. PR7—1F 25
Chelmsford Wlk. PR5—6C 14
Cheriton Field. PR2—4G 3
Cherry Clo. PR2—5D 4
Cherry Tree Clo. PR2—5D 4
Cherry Tree Gro. PR6—4G 21
Cherry Trees. PR5—2C 12
Cherry Wood. PR1—2E 10
Cherrywood Clo. PR5—6G 15
Chesham Dri. PR4—5D 10
Cheshire Ho. Clo. PR5—6K 11
Chesmere Dri. PR1—7F 7
Chester Av. PR7—4J 25
Chester Rd. PR1—3C 8
Chestnut Av. PR1—1E 10
Chestnut Av. PR6—5J 21
Chestnut Av. PR7—3A 20
Chestnut Cres. PR2—2E 8
Chestnut Dri. PR2—4H 3
Chestnuts, The. PR7—6D 24
Cheviot St. PR1—4H 7
Chiltern Av. PR7—6B 20
Chindits Way. PR2—7B 4
Chines, The. PR2—7J 3
Chisnall La. PR7—6H 23
Chorley Hall Rd. PR7—5G 21
Chorley La. PR7—6A 24
Chorley N. Ind. Est. PR6—4H 21
Chorley Old Rd. PR6
　　　　　—3G to 7F 17
Chorley Rd. PR5—1D 12
(Walton-le-Dale)
Chorley Rd. PR7 & PR6—6K 25
(Heath Charnock)
Chorley West Business Pk. PR7
　　　　　—7D 20
Christ Chu. St. PR1—5J 7
Christian Rd. PR1—5J 7
Church Av. PR1—6G 7
(Penwortham)
Church Av. PR1—4E 8
(Preston)
Church Brow. PR5—7D 8
Church Brow. PR7—7G 21
Churchfield. PR2—5K 3
Church Hill. PR6—7F 17
Churchill Rd. PR2—2H 3
Churchill Way. PR5—4J 15
Church La. PR3—2H 9
Church La. PR4 & PR5—6J 11
Church La. PR7—4A 24
Church La. PR5—6E 12 & 7F 13
(Bamber Bridge, in three parts)
Church Rd. PR5—6J 15
(Leyland)
Church Row. PR1—4A 8
Churchside. PR4—5D 10
Church St. PR1—5A 8
Church St. PR5—2H 13
(Higher Walton)
Church St. PR5—4K 15
(Leyland)
Church St. PR7—1G 25
Church Ter. PR5—2H 13
Church Wlk. PR7—7D 18
(Eccleston)
Church Wlk. PR7—5A 20
(Euxton)
Cinnamon Ct. PR1—3G 11
Cinnamon Hill Dri. N. PR5
　　　　　—2D 12
Cinnamon Hill Dri. S. PR5
　　　　　—2D 12
Cintra Av. PR2—1H 7
Cintra Ter. PR2—1H 7
Clairane Av. PR5—5J 3
Clancutt La. PR7—5C 24
Clanfield. PR2—4J 3
Clara St. PR1—5C 8
Claremont Av. PR5—6K 15

Claremont Av. PR7—1F 25
Claremont Rd. PR7—3F 25
Clarence St. PR5—4K 15
Clarence St. PR7—1H 25
Clarendon St. PR1—6A 8
Clarendon St. PR6—1J 25
Claugton Av. PR5—5C 16
Clayton Av. PR5—7F 15
Clayton Brook Rd. PR5—1F 17
Claytongate. PR7—6D 24
Clayton Grn. Rd. PR6—3E 16
Clayton's Ga. PR1—4K 7
Clayton St. PR5—4E 12
Clevedon Rd. PR2—7E 2
Cleveland Av. PR2—7C 4
Cleveland Rd. PR5—4H 15
Cleveland St. PR7—7G 21
(Chorley)
Cleveland St. PR7—7C 24
(Coppull)
Cleveleys Av. PR2—7G 3
Cleveleys Rd. PR5—2K 13
Cliff Dri. PR6—6F 17
Cliffe Ct. PR1—4D 8
Clifford St. PR7—7H 21
Cliff St. PR1—6J 7
Clifton Av. PR2—2E 6
Clifton Av. PR5—6K 15
Clifton Cres. PR1—1C 8
Clifton Dri. PR1—7G 7
Clifton Gro. PR7—1F 25
Clifton Ho. PR2—7C 4
Clifton Pde. PR5—3A 16
Clifton Pl. PR2—2F 7
Clifton St. PR1—6H 7
Clitheroe St. PR1—5C 8
Clive Rd. PR1—6F 7
Cloisters, The. PR2—4H 7
Close, The. PR2—5E 4
Close, The. PR4—6E 10
Clough Acre. PR7—5E 20
Clough Av. PR5—2B 12
Clovelly Av. PR2—1H 7
Clovelly Dri. PR1—7E 6
Cloverfield. PR1—1F 11
Clover Field. PR4—4F 17
Clover Rd. PR7—3E 24
Club St. PR5—6E 12
Clydesdale Pl. PR5—4E 14
Clyde St. PR2—4G 7
Cobden St. PR6—6J 21
Cocker Bar Rd. PR5—6A 14
Cocker La. PR5—5D 14
Cocker Rd. PR5—6G 13
Cockersand Av. PR4—4A 10
Cold Bath St. PR1—4J 7
Colebatch. PR2—6H 3
Colenso Rd. PR2—2G 7
College St. PR1—2K 7
Colliery St. PR7—1G 25
Collingwood Rd. PR7—1E 24
Collinson St. PR1—3C 8
Collins Rd. PR5—4E 12
Collins Rd. N. PR5—3F 13
Collison Av. PR7—7G 21
Colman Ct. PR1—6H 7
Colman St. PR1—6H 7
Colt Ho. Clo. PR5—7J 15
Colwyn Pl. PR2—1E 6
Colyton Clo. PR6—7J 21
Colyton Rd. PR6—7J 21
Colyton Rd. E. PR6—7J 21
Comet Rd. PR5—4E 14
Commercial Rd. PR7—6G 21
Common Bank Employment
        Area. PR7—1D 24
Common Bank La. PR7—1D 24
Compass Rd. PR2—4C 6
Compton Grn. PR2—4G 3
Conder Rd. PR2—3C 6
Congress St. PR7—6G 21
Coniston Av. PR2—2H 7
Coniston Av. PR7—6B 20
Coniston Dri. PR5—4D 12
Coniston Rd. PR2—7C 4

Coniston Rd. PR7—2F 25
Connaught Rd. PR1—7J 7
Constable Av. PR5—6A 12
Convent Clo. PR5—4D 12
  (Bamber Bridge)
Convent Clo. PR5—4A 16
  (Leyland)
Conway Av. PR1—4K 11
Conway Av. PR5—6A 16
Conway Clo. PR7—6C 20
Conway Dri. PR2—5G 3
Conway Rd. PR7—1E 22
Coombes, The. PR2—6K 3
Co-operative St. PR5—5E 12
Cooper Hill Clo. PR5—7D 8
Cooper Hill Dri. PR5—7D 8
Cooper Rd. PR1—5H 7
Cooper's La. PR7—7D 22
Coote La. PR4 & PR5
              —6J 11 to 5A 12
Cop La. PR1—7F 7 to 2G 11
Copperwood Way. PR7—1D 24
Coppice Clo. PR6—6J 21
Coppice, The. PR2—7F 3
Coppull Hall La. PR7—7E 24
Copse, The. PR7—4F 25
Copthurst La. PR6—1J 21
Corncroft. PR1—2G 11
Cornthwaite Rd. PR2—1J 7
Coronation Cres. PR1—5B 8
Corporation St. PR1
              —4K to 5K 7
Corporation St. PR6—6H 21
Cotswold Av. PR7—6B 20
Cotswold Clo. PR7—2F 23
Cotswold Ho. PR7—2G 25
Cotswold Rd. PR7—2G 25
Cottage Fields. PR7—3F 25
Cottage La. PR5—3F 13
Cottam Av. PR2—7E 2
Cottam Hall La. PR2—6C 2
Cottam La. PR2—2E to 1E 6
Cottam La. PR4—7A 10
Cottam St. PR7—2G 25
Cotton Ct. PR1—4A 8
Countess Way. PR5—4E 12
Countess Way. PR7—5B 20
Coupe Grn. PR5—1K 13
Couplands, The. PR7—7C 24
Court, The. PR1—1G 11
Court, The. PR2—4G 3
Coventry St. PR7—2G 25
Cow La. PR5—6H 15
Cowley Rd. PR2—7E 4
Cowling Brow. PR6—1J 25
Cowling Cotts. PR7—5B 24
Cowling La. PR5—5F 15
Cowling Rd. PR6—2K 25
Cow Well La. PR6—6F 17
Crabtree Av. PR1—2E 10
Cragg's Row. PR1—3K 7
Cranborne St. PR1—4C 8
Cranbourne Dri. PR6—1J 25
Cranbourne St. PR5—5E 12
Cranbourne St. PR6—1H 25
Craven Clo. PR2—4K 3
Crawford Av. PR1—3F 9
Crawford Av. PR5—6J 15
Crawford Av. PR7—1F 25
Crescent St. PR1—3C 8
Crescent, The. PR2—2E 6
  (Ashton-on-Ribble)
Crescent, The. PR2—3B 6
  (Lea)
Crescent, The. PR5—3F 13
  (Bamber Bridge)
Crescent, The. PR5—5C 12
  (Lostock Hall)
Crescent, The. PR7—5G 21
Cresswell St. PR2—1D 6
Croasdale Av. PR2—7E 4
Crocus Field. PR5—7J 15
Croft Bank. PR7—7D 22
Crofters Grn. PR1—2J 7
Crofters Grn. PR7—4A 20

Crofters Wlk. PR1—3H 11
Croftgate. PR2—6K 3
Croft Meadow. PR5—7J 13
Croft Rd. PR6—1J 25
Croft St. PR1—4H 7
Croft, The. PR7—1E 22
  (Eccleston)
Croft, The. PR7—4K 19
  (Euxton)
Crombleholme Rd. PR1—3E 8
Cromer Pl. PR2—7E 2
Cromford Wlk. PR1—4C 8
Crompton St. PR1—3C 8
Cromwell Av. PR1—2G 11
Cromwell Rd. PR1—2F 11
Cromwell Rd. PR2—7D 4
Cromwell St. PR1—3A 8
Crooked La. PR1—4A 8
Crookings La. PR1—6E 6
Crook St. PR1—4A 8
Crook St. PR7—3F 25
Crosby Pl. PR2—7E 2
Crosse Hall La. PR6—1J 25
Crosse Hall St. PR6—1K 25
Cross Field. PR4—4A 10
Cross Grn. Rd. PR2—5J 3
Cross Halls. PR2—1F 11
Cross St. PR1—5K 7
Cross St. PR5—4K 15
Cross St. PR7—6G 21
Cross Swords Clo. PR7—3E 24
Croston La. PR7—6K 23
Croston Rd. PR5
              —3G 15 to 5A 12
Crow Hills Rd. PR1—6E 6
Crowle St. PR1—4D 8
Crownlee. PR1—2E 10
Crown St. PR1—4K 7
Crown St. PR5—3K 15
Crown St. PR7—7G 21
Crummock Rd. PR1—3G 9
Cuerdale La. PR5—7F 9
Cuerden Av. PR5—7F 15
Cuerden Clo. PR5—2C 16
Cuerden Rise. PR5—6C 12
Cuerden St. PR6—1J 25
Cuerden Way. PR5—5D 12
Culbeck La. PR5—5H 19
Cumberland Av. PR5—7G 15
Cunliffe St. PR1—4A 8
Cunliffe St. PR7—1G 25
Cunnery Meadow. PR5—5C 16
Cunningham Av. PR7—2F 25
Curate St. PR6—6J 21
Curwen St. PR1—3C 8
  (in two parts)
Customs Way. PR2—4G 7
Cutt Clo. PR5—1B 18
Cuttle St. PR1—4D 8
Cyon Clo. PR5—1B 18
Cypress Clo. PR2—7G 5
Cypress Gro. PR5—5B 12

Dacca St. PR7—6H 21
  (in two parts)
Daisy Bank Clo. PR5—5F 15
Daisy Croft. PR2—4B 6
Daisyfields. PR4—4D 2
Daisy La. PR1—1C 8
Daisy Meadow. PR5—1F 17
Dakin St. PR7—1H 25
Dalby Clo. PR1—1D 8
Dale Av. PR7—6B 20
Dalehead Rd. PR5—7J 15
Dale St. PR1—4B 8
Dale View. PR7—4G 25
Dallas St. PR1—1J 7
Dalmore Rd. PR2—1E 6
Dane Hall La. PR7—5F 19
Danes Dri. PR5—4D 12
Danesway. PR1—1E 10
Danesway. PR5—4D 12
Danewerk St. PR1—4A 8
Darkinson La. PR4—7A 2

Dark La. L40—5A 22
Dark La. PR6—2J 21
Darlington St. PR7—7B 24
Dart St. PR2—2H 7
Darwen St. PR1—5C 8
Daub Hall La. PR5—4K 13
Dawber's La. PR7—5F 19
Dawlish Pl. PR2—1E 6
Dawnay Rd. PR2—1E 8
Dawson La. PR6 & PR5—7B 16
Dawson Pl. PR5—6G 13
Dawson Wlk. PR1—3K 7
Dean St. PR5—4E 12
Deborah Av. PR2—4A 4
Deepdale Mill St. PR1—3B 8
Deepdale Pk. PR1—2C 8
Deepdale Rd. PR1 & PR2
              —4b to 1B 8
Deepdale St. PR1—4B 8
Deerfold. PR7—5F 21
Deighton Av. PR5—6J 15
Deighton Rd. PR7—2F 25
De Lacy St. PR2—2H 7
Delamere Pl. PR6—7H 21
Delaware St. PR1—3C 8
Dell, The. PR2—4H 3
Dellway, The. PR4—2B 10
Delph La. PR7—2A to 4C 24
Demming Clo. PR2—4A 6
Denbigh Clo. PR5—5K 15
Denbigh Way. PR1—5A 8
Denby Clo. PR5—2C 12
Denford Av. PR5—6K 15
Denham La. PR6—5H 17
Denville Rd. PR1—3C 8
Derby Pl. PR6—7K 25
Derby Rd. PR2—7J 3
Derby Sq. PR1—4D 8
Derby St. PR1—4A 8
Derby St. PR5—4K 15
Derek Rd. PR6—5G 17
Derry Rd. PR2—1E 8
Derwent Rd. PR7—3F 25
Derwentwater Pl. PR2—2K 7
Dever Av. PR5—5F 15
Devon Clo. PR5—2D 12
Devon Ct. PR1—3D 8
Devonport Way. PR6—1J 25
Devonshire Ct. PR7—1G 25
Devonshire Pl. PR1—3E 8
Devonshire Rd. PR2—7A 4
Devonshire Rd. PR7—1G 25
Dewhurst Row. PR6—5D 12
Dewhurst St. PR2—3H 7
Dickensons Field. PR1—3J 11
Dickens Rd. PR7—7C 24
Dickson Av. PR1—2D 8
Dickson Hey. PR4—5D 10
Dickson St. PR1—5B 8
Dingle, The. PR4—4H 3
Dob Brow. PR7—4C 24
Doctor's La. PR7—2D 22
Dodd Way. PR5—7G 13
Dodgson Pl. PR1—3C 8
Dodgson Rd. PR1—3C 8
Dodney Dri. PR2—3A 6
Dole La. PR7—7G 21
Doll La. PR5—5C 14
Dolphin Brow. PR6—7F 17
Doodstone Av. PR5—4B 12
Doodstone Clo. PR5—4B 12
Doodstone Dri. PR5—4B 12
Doodstone Nook Rd. PR5
              —4B 12
Doris St. PR6—6H 21
Dorking Rd. PR6—3K 21
Dorman Rd. PR2—1E 8
Dorothy Av. PR5—5J 15
Dorset Av. PR5—2D 12
Dorset Rd. PR1—3A 8
Douglas Clo. PR5—6F 13
Douglas Ho. PR7—3F 25
Douglas Pl. PR7—3F 25
Douglas Rd. PR2—1H 7
Douglas Rd. N. PR2—1H 7

Douglas St. PR2—4G 7
Doultons, The. PR5—2C 12
Dove Av. PR1—1J 11
Dove Cote. PR6—3E 16
Dovedale Av. PR2—7E 2
Dovedale Clo. PR2—7E 2
Dovedale Clo. PR5—1J 19
Dovedale Ho. PR2—7E 2
Dove St. PR1—3B 8
Downham Pl. PR2—2C 6
Downham Rd. PR5—6E 14
Downing Ct. PR3—1G 3
Downing St. PR1—4E 8
Draper Av. PR7—2E 22
Draperfield. PR7—4E 24
Driscoll St. PR1—4B 8
Drive, The. PR5—7F 9
Drumacre La. E. PR4—7A 10
Drumacre La. W. PR4—7A 10
Drumhead Rd. PR6—4H 21
Duchy Av. PR2—7B 4
Ducie Pl. PR1—3F 9
Duck La. PR2—7H 3
Duddle La. PR5—4D 12
Dudley Pl. PR2—2D 6
Dukes Meadow. PR2—6E 2
Duke St. PR1—5B 8
Duke St. PR5—6E 12
Duke St. PR7—2G 25
Dunbar Dri. PR2—7H 3
Dunbar Rd. PR2—1D 6
Dundonald St. PR1—4D 8
Dunkirk Av. PR2—1G 7
Dunkirk La. PR5
—5B 14 to 6F 15
Dunmore St. PR1—4B 8
Dunoon Clo. PR2—7D 2
Dunrobin Dri. PR7—6B 20
Dunscar Dri. PR6—6J 21
Dunsop Clo. PR5—5F 13
Dunsop Rd. PR2—7D 4
Durham Clo. PR5—1G 19
Durton La. PR3—2J 3 to 2B 4
Duxbury Hall Rd. PR7—5J 25
Dymock Rd. PR1—3D 8
(in two parts)

Ealing Gro. PR6—4K 21
Earls Av. PR5—5E 12
Earl St. PR1—4K 7
Earls Way. PR7—5B 20
Earnshaw Bri. PR5—5F 15
Eastbourne Clo. PR2—6D 2
East Cliff. PR1—6K 7
E. Cliff Rd. PR1—6K 7
Eastgate. PR2—7J 3
Eastham St. PR1—3J 7
Eastlands. PR5—7E 14
Easton Clo. PR2—5D 4
East Rd. PR2—1A 8
East St. PR1—4A 8
East St. PR5—6E 12
(Bamber Bridge)
East St. PR5—4K 15
(Farington)
East St. PR5—5K 15
(Leyland)
East St. PR6—7H 21
East Ter. PR7—3B 20
East View. PR1—4A 8
East View. PR2—6F 5
East View. PR5—6A 12
(Lostock Hall)
East View. PR5—6C 8
(Walton-le-Dale)
Eastway. PR2—3G 3
Eastway Bus. Village. PR2
—4B 4
Eastwood Rd. PR5—5H 15
Eaves Grn. Rd. PR7—3F 25
Eaves La. PR6—6J 21 to 1J 25
Eccles St. PR1—3C 8
Ecroyd Rd. PR2—2G 7
Ecroyd St. PR5—5J 15

Edale Clo. PR5—7J 15
Edale Ct. PR1—3K 7
Eden St. PR5—6J 15
Edenway. PR2—4H 3
Edgefield. PR7—5F 21
Edgehill Clo. PR2—7J 3
Edgehill Cres. PR5—4G 15
Edgehill Dri. PR2—7H 3
Edinburgh Clo. PR5—5A 16
Edmund St. PR1—4B 8
Edward St. PR1—4K 7
Edward St. PR5—5E 12
(Bamber Bridge)
Edward St. PR5—6J 15
(Leyland)
Edward St. PR5—7C 8
(Walton-le-Dale)
Edward St. PR6—1H 25
Edward St. W. PR1—4J 7
Egan St. PR1—4A 8
Egbert St. PR1—3A 8
Egerton Gro. PR2—2F 25
Egerton Rd. PR2—3E 6
Egerton St. PR5—4H 15
Elbow St. PR7—1G 25
Elcho St. PR1—2A 8
Elder Clo. PR6—4G 17
Eldon Ho. PR2—1H 25
Eldon St. PR2 & PR1—2G 7
Eldon St. PR6—1H 25
Elgin St. PR1—2A 8
Elijah St. PR1—4D 8
Elizabeth St. PR1—4K 7
Ellen Ct. PR1—2K 7
Ellen St. PR1—3H to 2K 7
(in four parts)
Ellen St. PR5—4E 12
Ellerbeck Av. PR2—6E 4
Ellerslie Rd. PR2—3F 7
Elliot Clo. PR1—2J 7
Elliot St. PR1—2J 3 & 3J 7
Elliot Wlk. PR1—2J 7
Elm Av. PR2—2D 6
Elm Dri. PR5—4F 13
Elmfield Dri. PR5—7J 13
Elm Gro. PR2—2E 8
Elm Gro. PR5—3B 16
Elm Gro. PR6—5J 21
Elmsley St. PR1—1J 7
Elms, The. PR6—5G 17
Elmwood Av. PR5—5G 15
Elmwood Dri. PR1—1F 11
Elswick Clo. PR5—6F 15
Elswick Rd. PR2—3C 6
Elton St. PR2—3G 7
Emerson Rd. PR1—2D 8
Emily St. PR5—5A 12
Emily St. PR7—3F 25
Emmanuel St. PR1—2J 7
(in two parts)
Emmett St. PR1—3K 7
Emnie La. PR5—7E 14
Empress Av. PR2—7J 3
Empress Way. PR7—5C 20
Enfield Clo. PR7—3E 22
English Martyrs Pl. PR1—2K 7
Ennerdale Clo. PR5—7J 15
Ennerdale Dri. PR5—7E 8
Ennerdale Rd. PR7—3E 24
Ephraim St. PR1—5C 8
Epping Pl. PR6—7H 21
Epsom Clo. PR6—3K 21
Erskine Rd. PR6—6J 21
Esher Pond. PR2—5G 3
Eskdale Clo. PR2—3K 3
Eskdale Rd. PR5—7A 16
Esplanade. PR1—7B 8
Essex St. PR1—3A 8
Eton Pk. PR2—6C 4
Euston St. PR1—5J 7
Euxton Hall Gdns. PR7—5A 20
Euxton La. PR7—3B 20 to 4G 21
Evans St. PR2—3H 7
Evergreen Av. PR5—7J 15

Eversleigh St. PR1—3J 7
Evesham Av. PR1—3J 11
Evesham Clo. PR4—4A 10
Ewell Clo. PR6—3K 21
Exe St. PR1—2B 8
Exeter Pl. PR2—2C 6

Factory La. PR1—2J 11
Fairfax Pl. PR5—3D 12
Fairfax Rd. PR2—7E 4
Fairfield Dri. PR2—2F 7
Fairfield Rd. PR2—7A 4
Fairfield Rd. PR5—6H 15
Fairfield St. PR5—6B 12
Fairham Av. PR1—3H 11
Fairhaven Rd. PR1—7J 7
Fairhaven Rd. PR5—5F 15
Fair Oak Clo. PR2—1F 9
Fairsnape Rd. PR2—1G 9
Fairway. PR1—6F 7
Fairway. PR7—5G 21
Fairways. PR2—5A 4
Fairways Av. PR3—1G 3
Falcon St. PR1—2B 8
Falkland St. PR1—5J 7
Far Croft. PR5—4A 12
Far Field. PR1—1H 11
Far Nook. PR6—7F 17
Farington Clo. PR1—3F 9
Farington Cres. PR1—3F 9
Farington La. PR2—1F 9
Farington Pl. PR1—3F 9
Farington St. PR7—7G 21
Farthings, The. PR7—6D 20
Fazackerley St. PR2—3G 7
Fazakerley St. PR7—7G 21
Fell Clo. PR5—5F 13
Fellery St. PR7—7G 21
Fell View. PR2—1J 5
Fell View. PR6—2J 25
Fellway Clo. PR5—5C 12
Felstead St. PR1—4D 8
Fensway. PR4—3B 10
Fenton Rd. PR2—7C 4
Fermor Rd. PR1—3E 8
Fern Bank. PR6—4H 21
Fern Clo. PR5—5B 12
Ferndale Clo. PR5—7K 15
Fernleigh. PR5—6C 14
Fern Meadow. PR6—4G 17
Ferns, The. PR5—2B 12
Fernyhalgh Ct. PR2—5D 4
Fernyhalgh Gdns. PR2—5D 4
Fernyhalgh Gro. PR2—5D 4
Fernyhalgh La. PR2
—2C to 5D 4
Fernyhalgh Pl. PR2—5D 4
Ferrington St. PR2—4H 7
Fiddlers La. PR6—4F 17
Fidler La. PR5—1H 15
Fielden St. PR5—5F 15
Fielden St. PR6—7J 21
Fieldside Av. PR7—6A 20
Fields, The. PR7—1D 22
Fife Clo. PR6—2J 25
Filberts Clo. PR2—1G 7
Filberts, The. PR2—1G 7
File St. PR7—1G 25
Filey Pl. PR7—7E 2
Finch's Cotts. PR1—1J 11
Finch St. PR2—3A 6
Firbank. PR7—5A 20
First Av. PR2—2E 6
Fir Tree Av. PR2—7F 3
Fir Trees Av. PR7—7F 5
Fir Trees Av. PR5—4K 11
Fir Trees Cres. PR5—5A 12
Fir Trees Pl. PR2—7F 5
Fir Trees Rd. PR5—4A 12
Fishergate. PR1—5K 7
(in two parts)
Fishergate Hill. PR1—6J 7

Fishergate Shopping Cen. PR1
—5K 7
Fishergate Wlk. PR1—5K 7
(off St George's Cen.)
Fisher St. PR1—4C 8
Fish St. PR1—3K 7
Fishwick Pde. PR1—4C 8
Fishwick Rd. PR1—4C 8
Fishwick View. PR1—4C 8
Fitchfield. PR1—3K 11
Fitzgerald St. PR1—5H 7
Fitzroy St. PR1—5H 7
Five Acres. PR5—2G 15
Flag La. PR1—5J 11
Flag La. PR5 & PR7—3F 19
Flag La. PR6—3K 25
Flats, The. PR7—2F 25
Fleet St. PR1—5K 7
Fleet St. PR7—1G 25
Fleetwood St. PR2—3H 7
Fleetwood St. PR5—4K 15
Flensburg Way. PR5
—3F 15 to 7J 11
Fletcher Rd. PR1—4B 8
Flett St. PR2—3G 7
Floyd Rd. PR2—1E 8
Floyer St. PR1—5B 8
Foregate. PR2—7J 3
Forest Brook Ho. PR2—1K 7
Forest Clo. PR5—2C 20
Forest Way. PR2—6K 3
Forest Way. PR5—6H 15
Forge St. PR5—5J 15
Formby Pl. PR2—2C 6
(in two parts)
Forrester Clo. PR5—5G 15
Forshaw Rd. PR1—3H 11
Forton Rd. PR2—4C 6
Fossdale Moss. PR5—5E 14
Foster Croft. PR1—6G 7
Fosterfield Pl. PR6—6J 21
Foster St. PR6—6J 21
Foundary St. PR7—7G 21
Fountains Clo. PR7—3H 25
Fourfields. PR5—3E 12
Four Oaks Rd. PR5—7G 13
Fowler Av. PR5—7B 12
Fowler La. PR5—7K 11 to 1K 15
Fowler St. PR2—1H 7
Foxcote. PR7—5F 21
Foxdale Gro. PR1—1D 8
Foxhole Rd. PR7—6D 20
Fox La. PR5—6F 15
Fox St. PR1—5K 7
Francis St. PR2—3G 7
Franklands Dri. PR2—6F 5
Frank St. PR1—3K 7
Fraser Av. PR7—7J 7
Frederick St. PR6—1J 25
Freeman's La. PR7—5C 24
Frenchwood Av. PR1—6B 8
Frenchwood Knoll. PR1—6B 8
Frenchwood St. PR1—6A 8
Fresh Fields. PR7—1B 6
Friargate. PR1—4K to 5K 7
Friars, The. PR7—7J 3
Friday St. PR6—7H 21
Frome St. PR1—3D 8
Froom St. PR6—7J 21
Fryer Clo. PR1—3H 11
Fulford Av. PR2—3A 6
Fulshaw Rd. PR2—2F 7
Fulwood Hall La. PR2—7B 4
Fulwood Heights. PR2—6C 4
Fulwood Row. PR2—4E & 5E 4
Furness Clo. PR7—3H 25
Fylde Av. PR5—2G 15
Fylde Rd. PR2 & PR1—3H 7
Fylde St. PR1—4J 7

Gainsborough Av. PR5—6A 12
Gamull La. PR2—6F 5
Ganton Ct. PR1—6E 6
Garden St. PR1—5K 7

Garden St. PR5—6B 12
Garden St. PR7—6G 21
Garden Ter. PR7—6G 21
Garden Wlk. PR2—3F 7
Gardner St. PR1—4K 7
Garfield Ter. PR6—5H 21
Garrison Rd. PR2—1B 8
Garsdale Clo. PR5—7E 8
Garsdale Rd. PR2—7E 4
Garstang Rd. PR2 & PR1
—3H 3 to 2K 7
Garstang Rd. PR3—1G 3
Garstone Croft. PR2—5H 3
Gaskell Rd. PR1—7J 7
Gaskell St. PR6—7J 21
Gas Ter. PR5—4J 15
Gatesgarth Av. PR2—4K 3
Gathurst Rd. PR2—2G 7
Gaythorne Av. PR1—3F 9
Geneva Rd. PR2—7C 4
Geoffrey St. PR1—3C 8
Geoffrey St. PR6—6H 21
George's Rd. PR1—5K 7
George St. PR1—5B 8
George St. PR5—4K 15
George St. PR7—1G 25
German La. PR7
—7B 20 to 1C 24
(Charnock Richard)
German La. PR7—7C 24
(Coppull)
Gerrard St. PR1—5H 7
Gilbertson Rd. PR7—6J 25
Gilbert St. PR7—2G 25
Gildow St. PR1—4J 7
Gilhouse Av. PR2—3A 6
Gillcroft. PR7—1D 22
Giller Dri. PR1—3J 11
Giller Fold. PR1—3K 11
Gillett St. PR1—3C 8
(in two parts)
Gillibrand St. PR5—7D 8
Gillibrand St. PR7—1G 25
Gillibrand Walks. PR7—2F 25
Gill La. PR4—1A 14
Gin Bow. PR7—2H 25
Ginnel, The. PR5—6J 15
Gisburn Rd. PR2—7E 4
Glamis Dri. PR7—7F 21
Glamis Rd. PR5—6A 16
Glebe Clo. PR7—7K 3
Glencroft. PR7—4K 19
Glendale Av. PR5—4C 12
Glendale Clo. PR5—7K 15
Glendale Cres. PR5—4C 12
Glendale Gro. PR2—2D 8
Gleneagles Dri. PR1—6E 6
Gleneagles Dri. PR2—4F 3
Glen Gro. PR2—6F 5
Glenluce Dri. PR1—4F 9
Glenmore. PR6—3E 16
Glen, The. PR2—2F 9
Glenway. PR1—1G 11
Gloucester Av. PR5—3A 16
Gloucester Rd. PR2—2G 25
Glover Clo. PR5—1B 18
Glovers Ct. PR1—5K 7
Glover St. PR1—5A 8
Golbourne St. PR1—3B 8
Goldburn Clo. PR2—5D 2
Golden Hill. PR5—4K 15
Golden Hill La. PR5—4G 15
Goldfinch St. PR1—2B 8
Golf View. PR7—5E 2
Goodier St. PR1—4C 8
Good St. PR1—5J 7
Goodwood Av. PR2—4K 3
Goose Grn. Av. PR7—7D 24
Gordon St. PR1—3J 7
(in two parts)
Gordon St. PR6—1H 25
Goring St. PR7—1H 25
Gorse Clo. PR2—2J 11
Gorse Gro. PR2—1E 8
Gorsewood Rd. PR5—5G 15

Gough La. PR5—7H 13 to 1G 17
Goulding Av. PR5—5K 15
Goulding St. PR7—2H 25
Gradwell St. PR1—4J 7
Grafton Rd. PR2—7F 5
Grafton St. PR1—6J 7
Grafton St. PR7—3F 25
Graham Av. PR5—5C 12
Graham St. PR1—3B 8
Grange Av. PR2—7F 5
Grange Dri. PR5—1K 13
Grange Dri. PR7—3A 20
Grange Pk. Clo. PR1—6E 6
Grange Pl. PR2—7F 5
Grange Rd. PR2—1G 7
Grange Rd. PR5—5F 15
Granton Wlk. PR2—7E 2
Granville Ct. PR6—6J 21
Granville Rd. PR6—6J 21
Grasmere Av. PR5—3J 15
Grasmere Clo. PR2—7C 4
Grasmere Clo. PR5—3E 12
Grasmere Clo. PR7—6C 20
Grasmere Gro. PR6—7F 17
Grasmere Ter. PR7—3F 25
Gt. Avenham St. PR1—6A 8
Gt. George St. PR1—3A 8
Gt. Greens La. PR5—1F 17
Gt. Hanover St. PR1—3A 8
Gt. Meadow. PR5—5A 12
Gt. Meadow. PR7—5E 20
Gt. Shaw St. PR1—4K 7
Gt. Townley St. PR1—4D 8
Greaves Meadow. PR1—4J 11
Greaves St. PR1—5A 8
Greaves Town La. PR2—3C 6
Greenacres. PR2—4F 3
Greenacres, The. PR4—3B 10
Greenbank Av. PR1—2H 7
Greenbank Pl. PR1—3J 7
Greenbank Rd. PR1—1J 11
Greenbank St. PR1—2H to 3J 7
(in three parts)
Greencroft. PR1—2H 11
Green Dri. PR1—7F 7
Green Dri. PR2—4J 3
Green Dri. PR5—4C 12
Greenfield Dri. PR5—5A 12
Greenfield Rd. PR6—7J 21
Greenfield Way. PR2—6F 3
Green Ga. PR2—1G 7
Green Ga. PR4—4A 10
Greenlands Cres. PR2—1E 8
Greenlands Gro. PR2—1E 8
Green La. PR4—4G 11
Green La. PR7—7E 24
Green Pl. PR5—7G 13
Greenside. PR7—4A 20
Greenside Av. PR2—3A 6
Greenside Gdns. PR5—7D 14
Green St. PR1—5J 7
Green St. PR7—3E 24
Greensway. PR3—1G 3
Green, The. PR2—2F 9
Green, The. PR6—6K 25
Green, The. PR7—2E 22
Greenthorn Cres. PR2—2G 9
Greenway. PR1—1F 11
Greenway. PR2—4H 3
Greenway. PR7—1D 22
Greenwood. PR5—1F 17
Greenwood Ct. PR5—4J 15
Greenwood St. PR1—5B 8
Greenwood St. PR5—4E 12
Gregson La. PR5—2H 13
Gregson Way. PR2—6B 4
Grenville Av. PR5—3D 12
Greyfriars Av. PR2—6H 3
Greyfriars Cres. PR2—6H 3
Greyfriars Dri. PR1—7G 7
Grey Heights View. PR6—7J 21
Greystock Av. PR2—5J 3
Greystock Clo. PR5—5H 13
Greystock Pl. PR2—5J 3
Greystones. PR5—5D 14

Grime St. PR7—2H 25
Grimsargh St. PR1—3D 8
Grimshaw St. PR1—5A 8
Grisdale Pl. PR7—3C 25
Grizedale Clo. PR2—2F 9
Grizedale Cres. PR2—2F 9
Grizedale Pl. PR2—2F 9
Grosvenor Pl. PR2—2F 7
Grosvenor Rd. PR7—2F 25
Grosvenor St. PR1—5B 8
Grove Rd. PR5—6C 8
Grove St. PR5—5F 13
(Bamber Bridge)
Grove St. PR5—6F 15
(Leyland)
Grove, The. PR1—1F 11
Grove, The. PR2—3F 7
Grove, The. PR7—5G 21
Grundy's La. PR7—7G & 6G 25
Grundy St. PR5—4J 15
Guildford Av. PR6—3J 21
Guildford Rd. PR1—5A 8
Guildhall St. PR1—5K 7
Guild Row. PR1—5A 8
Guy's Clo. PR1—4A 8

Hacklands Av. PR2—3A 6
Haddon Pl. PR2—1H 7
Haig Av. PR2—2H 7
Haig Av. PR5—5H 15
Haigh Clo. PR7—1E 24
Haigh Cres. PR1—1F 25
Haighton Ct. PR2—4A 4
Haighton Grn. La. PR2—2C 4
Half Acre. PR5—5A 12
Halfpenny La. PR7—5C 22
Hall Croft. PR4—3B 10
Hall Croft Head. PR4—3B 10
Hall Ga. PR7—6E 20
Hall Grn. La. L40—5C 22
Halliwell Ct. PR7—1G 25
(off Halliwell St.)
Halliwell La. PR6—3G 21
Halliwell St. PR7—1G 25
Hall La. L40—5A 22
Hall Rd. PR1—2J 11
Hall Rd. PR2—6J 3
Hall St. PR2—3G 7
Hallwood Rd. PR7—3E 24
Halsbury St. PR1—6B 8
Halstead Rd. PR2—6D 4
Halton Av. PR5—4B 16
Halton Pl. PR2—7F 5
Hambledon Dri. PR1—3J 11
Hamer Rd. PR2—1H 7
Hamilton Gro. PR2—1E 8
Hamilton Rd. PR2—7D 4
Hamilton Rd. PR7—1F 25
Hammond Ct. PR1—3J 7
Hammond's Row. PR1—5A 8
Hammond St. PR1—3J to 2K 7
(in three parts)
Hampden Rd. PR5—4J 15
Hampson Av. PR5—5B 16
Hampstead Rd. PR2—2D 8
Hampton Clo. PR7—7F 21
Hampton St. PR2—2G 7
Hanbury St. PR2—3G 7
Handbridge, The. PR2—6J 3
Hand La. L40—3B 22
Hanover Ct. PR2—5D 2
Hanover St. PR1—3K 7
Harcourt St. PR1—3J 7
Hardacre La. PR6—2F 21
Hardcastle Rd. PR2—1J 7
Hardman's Yd. PR1—5K 7
Hardwen Av. PR2—3A 6
Hardwick St. PR1—4A 8
Hardy Dri. PR7—1E 24
Hareden Clo. PR5—5F 13
Hareden Rd. PR2—2F 9
Harestone Av. PR7—3E 24
Harewood. PR7—5F 21

Harewood Rd. PR1—2B 8
Hargreaves Av. PR5—6K 15
Hargreaves Ct. PR2—7D 2
Harland St. PR2—1H 7
Harlech Dri. PR5—5A 16
Harling Rd. PR1—3D 8
Harold Ter. PR5—5A 12
Harperley. PR7—5F 21
Harpers La. PR7 & PR6—6H 21
Harpers St. PR7—5H 21
Harrington Rd. PR7—7F 21
Harrington St. PR1—4J 7
Harris Cen. PR2—6J 3
Harrison La. PR4—3F 11
Harrison Rd. PR2—6J 3
Harrison Rd. PR7—2G 25
Harris St. PR1—5A 8
Harrock Rd. PR5—5B 16
Harrop Pl. PR2—7E 4
Hartington Rd. PR1—5H 7
Hartwood Grn. PR6—4H 21
Hassett Clo. PR1—6J 7
Hastings Rd. PR2—3F 7
Hastings Rd. PR5—4K 15
Hatfield Rd. PR2—1E 8
Havelock Rd. PR1—7J 7
Havelock Rd. PR5—6E 12
Havelock St. PR1—2H to 1K 7
(in four parts)
Hawarden Rd. PR1—3E 8
Haweswater Av. PR7—2F 25
Hawkhurst Av. PR2—5H 3
Hawkhurst Cres. PR2—5H 3
Hawkhurst Rd. PR1—1J 11
(Penwortham)
Hawkhurst Rd. PR1—3B 8
(Preston)
Hawkins Clo. PR1—3J 7
Hawkins St. PR1—3J 7
(in two parts)
Hawksbury Dri. PR1—3H 11
Hawkshead. PR1—2J 11
Hawkshead Av. PR7—6B 20
Hawkshead Rd. PR2—6K 8
Hawkswood. PR7—2D 22
Hawthorn Clo. PR4—6E 10
Hawthorn Clo. PR5—4F 15
Hawthorn Cres. PR2—3B 6
Hawthorne Av. PR5—2J 13
Hawthorne Clo. PR6—3F 17
Hawthorn Rd. PR2—2E 8
Hawthorns, The. PR2—5K 3
Hawthorns, The. PR1—1D 22
Haydock Av. PR5—6J 15
Haydock Rd. PR5—3E 12
Haydon Av. PR5—6A 12
Hayfield Av. PR5—4K 13
Hayling Pl. PR2—7E 2
Haysworth St. PR1—2K 7
Hazel Av. PR5—4G 13
Hazel Clo. PR1—2F 11
Hazel Clo. PR5—4F 13
Hazel Coppice. PR2—1C 6
Hazel Gro. PR2—7G 5
Hazel Gro. PR5—4F 13
Hazel Gro. PR6—4G 21
Hazelhurst Rd. PR2—2G 9
Hazelmere Rd. PR2—3E 6
(Ashton-on-Ribble)
Hazelmere Rd. PR2—3H 3
(Fulwood)
Hazels, The. PR7—7C 24
Hazelwood Clo. PR5—5G 15
Headley Rd. PR5—5G 15
Heald Ho. Rd. PR5—7A 16
Heald St. PR6—7J 21
Healey View. PR6—5J 21
Heapey Rd. PR6—5K 21
Heather Gro. PR2—1E 8
Heathers, The. PR2—2G 17
Heathfield. PR6—7K 25
Heathfield Dri. PR2—7E 4
Heathrow Pl. PR7—1E 24
Heathway. PR2—5K 3
Heatley St. PR1—4K 7

Heaton Clo. PR5—1D 12
Heaton Mt. Av. PR2—4K 3
Heaton Pl. PR1—3E 8
Heaton St. PR5—4G 15
Hellifield. PR2—4K 3
Henderson St. PR1—2J 7
Hendon Pl. PR2—2C 6
Hennel La. PR5—3B 12
Henrietta St. PR1—4B 8
Herbert St. PR1—3B 8
Herbert St. PR5—5J 15
Hermon St. PR1—3C 8
(in two parts)
Hern Av. PR5—5A 12
Herschell St. PR1—6A 8
Hesketh Rd. PR2—3E 8
Hesketh St. PR2—3G 7
Heversham Av. PR2—4K 3
Hewitt St. PR5—4K 15
Hewlett Av. PR7—7B 24
Hewlett St. PR7—7C 24
Hey End. PR4—5D 10
Heyes, The. PR6—4F 17
Heysham St. PR1—3J 7
Heys, The. PR7—6D 24
Heywood Rd. PR2—2C 6
Higford St. PR1—4B 8
High Cop. PR6—2K 17
Higher Bank Rd. PR2—1K 7
Higher Croft. PR1—3G to 4H 11
Higher Greenfield. PR2—6F 3
Higher Meadow. PR5—5C 16
Higher Walton Rd. PR5—7D 8
Highfield. PR1—3H 11
Highfield Av. PR2—7C 4
Highfield Av. PR5—3A 16
(Leyland)
Highfield Av. PR5—4C 12
(Lostock Hall)
Highfield Dri. PR1—3H 11
Highfield Dri. PR2—3J 3
Highfield Gro. PR5—3C 12
Highfield Ind. Est. PR7—5H 21
Highfield Rd. PR5—5A 18
Highfield Rd. N. PR7—5G 21
Highfield Rd. S. PR7—6G 21
Highgale Gdns. PR5—6C 12
Highgate. PR1—7F 7
Highgate Av. PR2—7J 3
Highgate Clo. PR2—7K 3
High Grn. PR5—5H 15
Highgrove Av. PR7—4H 23
Highgrove Ct. PR5—6B 14
Highgrove Ho. PR7—5G 21
Highland Av. PR1—1F 11
Highrigg Dri. PR3—2K 3
High St. Chorley, PR7—7G 21
High St. Preston, PR1—4A 8
Highways Av. PR7—6B 20
Hillbrook Grn. PR5—4H 15
Hillbrook Rd. PR5—4H 15
Hill Crest Av. PR2—3J 3
(Fulwood)
Hillcrest Av. PR2—7E 2
(Ingol)
Hillcroft. PR2—4G 3
Hillpark Av. PR2—7H 3
Hillpark Av. PR5—4K 13
Hill Rd. PR1—7G 7
Hill Rd. PR5—5A 16
Hill Rd. S. PR1—2G 11
Hillside. PR6—6G 17
Hillside Av. PR2—7H 3
Hillside Av. PR5—6K 11
Hillside Clo. PR7—6A 20
Hillside Cres. PR6—6G 17
Hillside Rd. PR1—6C 8
Hill St. PR1—4K 7
Hill St. PR7—7G 21
Hill Top. PR4—7E 10
Hill Top La. PR6—6G 17
Hill View Dri. PR7—7B 24
Hill Wlk. PR5—4J 15
Hindley St. PR7—2G 25
Hind St. PR1—6J 7

Hodder Av. PR7—3F 25
Hodder Clo. PR5—5F 13
Hodson St. PR5—4E 12
Hogg's La. PR7—3J 25
Hoghton La. PR5—2H 13
Hoghton St. PR5—5A 12
Hoghton View. PR1—6C 8
Holcombe Gro. PR6—6J 21
Holker Clo. PR5—2K 13
Holker La. PR5—3C 18
Holland Av. PR5—3E 12
Holland Rd. PR2—3G 7
Hollings. PR4—6D 10
Hollinhead Cres. PR2—7F 3
Hollinhurst Av. PR1—6G 7
Hollins Gro. PR2—1F 7
Hollinshead St. PR7—7G 21
Hollins La. PR5—3E 18
Hollins Rd. PR1—2B 8
Hollybank Clo. PR2—6D 2
Holly Clo. PR6—4F 17
Holly Cres. PR7—6C 24
Holly Pl. PR5—6H 13
Hollywood Av. PR1—2G 11
Holman St. PR1—3C 8
Holme Rd. PR1—5G 7
Holme Rd. PR5—5D 12
Holmes Ct. PR1—1J 7
Holme Slack La. PR1—1C 8
Holmes Meadow. PR5—5D 14
Holmfield Cres. PR2—3B 6
Holmfield Rd. PR2—7A 4
Holmrook Rd. PR1—3B 8
Holstein St. PR1—4A 8
Holt Av. PR7—6D 24
Holt Brow. PR5—1J 19
Holt La. PR6—3H 17
Homestead. PR5—2F 17
Homestead Clo. PR5—5F 15
Honeysuckle Row. PR2—2E 8
Hope St. PR1—4K 7
Hope St. PR7—6G 21
Hope Ter. PR5—5A 12
Hopwood St. PR1—4A 8
Hopwood St. PR5—5E 12
Hornbeam Clo. PR1—2F 11
Hornby Av. PR2—7E 4
Hornby Croft. PR5—6D 14
Hornby Rd. PR6—2J 25
Hornby St. PR1—4B 8
Hornchurch Dri. PR7—7E 20
Hornsea Clo. PR2—7E 2
Hough La. PR5—5J 15
Houghton Clo. PR1—2H 11
Houghton Rd. PR2—1G 11
Houghton Rd. PR5—5F 15
Houghton St. PR6—7H 21
Houldsworth Rd. PR2—1J 7
Howard Rd. PR7—3F 25
Howarth Rd. PR2—1H 7
Howe Gro. PR7—1E 24
Howgills, The. PR2—4A 4
Howick Cross La. PR1—7B 6
Howick Moor La. PR1—2D 10
Howick Pk. Av. PR1—1D 10
Howick Pk. Clo. PR1—1D 10
Howick Pk. Dri. PR1—1D 10
Hoylake Clo. PR2—5F 3
Hoyles La. PR4—6A 2
Hudson Ct. PR5—6J 13
Hudson St. PR1—6A 8
Hugh Barn La. PR4—6C 10
Hugh La. PR5—3E 14
Hull St. PR2—4G 7
Hunniball Ct. PR2—2G 7
Hunters Rd. PR5—5B 16
Hunts Field. PR6—4G 17
Hunt St. PR1—5H 7
Hurn Gro. PR7—1E 24
Hurst Brook. PR7—7D 24
Hurst Pk. PR1—1G 11
Hurstway. PR2—4H 3
Hurstway Clo. PR2—4H 3

Hutton Hall Av. PR4—4C 10

Iddesleigh Rd. PR1—3E 8
Illingworth Rd. PR1—3E 8
Ince La. PR7—3E 22
Ingleborough Way. PR5—5A 16
Ingle Head. PR2—5H 3
Ingleton Rd. PR2—7E 4
Ingot St. PR1—4H 7
Inkerman St. PR2—1G 7
Inskip Rd. PR2—3C 6
Inskip Rd. PR5—4F 15
Ipswich Rd. PR2—2D 8
Irongate. PR5—5C 12
Ironside Clo. PR2—7B 4
Irvin St. PR1—3B 8
Isherwood St. PR1—3C 8
Isleworth Dri. PR7—1F 25

Jackson Rd. PR5—5F 15
Jackson Rd. PR7—3E 24
Jackson St. PR5—5F 13
Jackson St. PR7—2H 25
Jacson St. PR1—5A 8
James Pl. PR7—7B 24
James St. PR1—5B 8
James St. PR5—4E 12
Jane La. PR5—3C 14
Janice Dri. PR2—4H 3
Jasmine Clo. PR2—5D 4
Jemmett St. PR1—2J 7
Johnspool. PR2—5G 3
John St. PR5—4E 12
(Bamber Bridge)
John St. PR5—5J 15
(Leyland)
John St. PR7—2G 25
(Chorley)
John St. PR7—7C 24
(Coppull)
John William St. PR1—4C 8
Jordan St. PR1—5J 7
Jubilee Av. PR2—3B 6
Jubilee Ct. PR5—6G 15
Jubilee Rd. PR5—5A 12
Judd Ho. PR1—6J 7
Judeland. PR7—5E 20
Juniper Croft. PR6—5E 16
Jutland St. PR1—4A 8

Kane St. PR2—3G 7
Kay St. PR1—5J 7
Keats Clo. PR7—3F 23
Kellet Acre. PR5—6A 12
Kellet Av. PR5—5B 16
Kellet La. PR5—7H 13
Kellett St. PR7—7G 21
Kem Mill La. PR6—6F 17
Kendal Ho. PR1—5A 8
Kendal St. PR1—4J 7
(in two parts)
Kenmure Pl. PR1—2K 7
Kennet Dri. PR2—3K 3
Kennington Rd. PR2—7A 4
Kensington Av. PR1—6F 7
Kensington Rd. PR1—1F 25
Kent Av. PR5—2D 12
Kent Dri. PR5—4B 16
Kentmere Av. PR5—4D 12
(Bamber Bridge)
Kentmere Av. PR5—3J 15
(Leyland)
Kent St. PR1—2K 7
Kenyon La. PR6—7K 17
Kershaw St. PR6—6J 21
Keswick Rd. PR2—2F 9
Kew Gdns. PR1—6F 7
Kew Gdns. PR5—3K 15
Kidlington Clo. PR5—5D 12
Kidsgrove. PR2—6D 8
Kilmuir Clo. PR2—6C 4
Kilncroft. PR6—3F 17

Kilngate. PR5—2C 12
Kilruddery Rd. PR1—7J 7
Kilshaw St. PR1—3K 7
Kilworth Height. PR2—6G 3
Kimberley Rd. PR2—-2G 7
Kimberley St. PR7—7C 24
Kingfisher St. PR1—2B 8
Kingsbridge Clo. PR1 -4J 11
Kings Ct. PR5—5J 15
Kings Cres. PR5—5J 15
Kingscroft. PR5—7D 8
Kingsdale Av. PR2—7D 4
Kingsdale Clo. PR5—1K 19
(Leyland)
Kingsdale Clo. PR5—7F 9
(Walton-le-Dale)
Kings Dri. PR2—6H 3
Kingsfold Dri. PR1—3G 11
Kingshaven Dri. PR1—3J 11
Kingsley Dri. PR7—3E 24
King St. PR5—5J 15
(Leyland)
King St. PR5—5B 12
(Lostock Hall)
King St. PR7—2H 25
Kingsway. PR1—6F 7
Kingsway. PR2—2D 6
Kingsway. PR5—5E 12
(Bamber Bridge)
Kingsway. PR5—7G 15
(Leyland)
Kingsway. PR7—5C 20
Kingsway Av. PR3—1G 3
Kingsway W. PR1—6E 6
Kingswood Rd. PR5—4J 15
Kingswood Dri. PR1—5J 7
Kirkby Av. PR5—5C 16
Kirkham Clo. PR5—5F 15
Kirkham St. PR1—4J 7
Kirkland Pl. PR2—4C 6
Kirkstall Clo. PR7—3H 25
Kirkstall Dri. PR7—3H 25
Kirkstall Rd. PR7—3H 25
Kirkstone Rd. PR2—2F 9
Kittingbourne Brow. PR5
—2G 13
Knot Acre. PR4—5E 10
Knot La. PR5—7E 8
Knowles St. PR1—4D 8
Knowles St. PR7—2G 25
Knowley Brow. PR6—5J 21
Knowsley Av. PR5—2A 16
Knowsley Rd. PR5—6A 16
Knowsley St. PR1—5A 8
Korea Rd. PR2—6B 4

Laburnham Dri. PR2—3H 3
Laburnum Av. PR5—5B 12
Laburnum Clo. PR1—1C 8
Laburnum Rd. PR6—4G 21
Lacy Av. PR1—3J 11
Lady Crosse Dri. PR6—7G 17
Lady Hey Cres. PR2—3A 6
Ladyman St. PR1—5J 7
Lady Pl. PR5—1E 12
Ladysmith Rd. PR2—2G 7
Lady St. PR1—4K 7
Ladywell St. PR1—4J 7
Lambert Clo. PR2—1E 8
Lambert Rd. PR2—1D 8
Lancaster Av. PR5—5C 16
Lancaster Ct. PR7—5G 21
Lancastergate. PR5—6H 15
Lancaster Ho. PR5—3J 15
Lancaster La. PR5—5B 16
Lancaster Rd. PR1
—4K 7 to 5A 8
Lancaster Rd. N. PR1—3K 7
Lancaster St. PR7—7D 24
Land La. PR5—4B 10
Landseer St. PR1—3C 8
Langcliffe Rd. PR2—7E 4
Langdale Clo. PR5—4D 12
Langdale Ct. PR1—1G 11

Langdale Cres. PR2—1E 8
Langdale Gro. PR6—7F 17
Langdale Rd. PR2—1E 8
Langdale Rd. PR5—1J 19
Langden Cres. PR5—6F 13
Langden Dri. PR2—1G 9
Langden Fold. PR2—1K 5
Langfield Clo. PR2—3K 3
Langholme Clo. PR5—6F 15
Langholme Rd. PR1—1E 10
Langport Clo. PR2—3K 3
Langton Brow. PR7—3E 22
Langton Clo. PR5—6E 14
Langton St. PR1—5H 7
Lansdown Hill. PR2—3G 3
Larch Av. PR6—5J 21
Larches Av. PR2—3D 6
Larches La. PR2—3C 6
Larch Gro. PR5—4F 13
Larchwood. PR1—1F 11
Larchwood. PR2—3C 6
Larchwood Cres. PR5—5G 15
Lark Av. PR1—1J 11
Larkfield. PR7—2D 22
Lark Hill. PR5—1H 13
Larkhill Rd. PR1—5B 8
Larkhill St. PR1—5B 8
Latham St. PR1—6A 8
Latham St. PR7—1H 25
Latimer Dri. PR4—5D 10
Lauderdale Cres. PR2—7F 5
Lauderdale Rd. PR2—7F 5
Lauderdale St. PR1—6J 7
Laund, The. PR5—5C 14
Laurel Av. PR7—4K 19
Laurel Bank Av. PR2—1G 7
Laurel St. PR1—5A 8
Lavender Clo. PR2—5C 4
Lawnwood Av. PR7—3E 24
Lawrence Av. PR1—7B 8
Lawrence Av. PR5—3D 12
Lawrence La. PR7—1E 22
Lawrence Rd. PR1—7F 7
Lawrence Rd. PR7—1F 25
Lawrence St. PR2—1H 7
Lawson St. PR1—4K 7
Lawson St. PR6—1J 25
Laxey Gro. PR1—7D 4
Layton Rd. PR2—3C 6
Leadale. PR2—2B 6
Leadale Grn. PR5—5G 15
Leadale Rd. PR5—5F 15
Leagram Cres. PR2—1G 9
Lea Rd. PR4 & PR2—7A 2
Lea Rd. PR6—2G 21
Leech Pl. PR5—5H 13
Leek St. PR1—4E 8
Leeson Av. PR7—4B 24
Leeward Rd. PR2—4D 6
Leicester Rd. PR1—3A 8
Leige Rd. PR5—6J 15
Leigh Brow. PR5—3B 12
Leigh Row. PR7—1G 25
Leigh St. PR7—1G 25
Leighton St. PR1—4J 7
Lennon St. PR1—1G 25
Lennox St. PR1—5A 8
Letchworth Dri. PR7—2F 25
Letchworth Pl. PR7—2F 25
Levens Dri. PR5—4B 16
Levensgarth Av. PR2—4K 3
Levens St. PR1—3D 8
Lever Ho. La. PR5—4A 16
Lex St. PR1—4C 8
Leyburn Clo. PR2—6E 4
Leyfield. PR1—3H 11
Leyfield Rd. PR5—5H 15
Leyland La. PR5
    —5E 18 to 4G 15
Leyland Rd. PR1 & PR5
    —7H 7 to 5A 12
Leyland St. PR2—4H 7
Leyland Way. PR5—5K 15
Leyton Av. PR5—7F 15
Leyton Grn. PR5—7G 15

Library Rd. PR6—2F 17
Library St. PR1—5A 8
Library St. PR7—1G 25
Lichen Clo. PR7—4B 24
Lichfield Rd. PR2—2D 6
Lichfield Rd. PR7—2F 25
Lidget Av. PR2—3A 6
Lightfoot Clo. PR2—3H 3
Lightfoot Grn. La. PR4—3F 3
Lightfoot La. PR2—4F to 3H 3
Lightfoot La. PR4—4D 2
Lighthurst Av. PR7—2G 25
Lighthurst La. PR7—3H 25
Lilac Av. PR1—3K 11
Lilac Gro. PR1—1C 8
Lily Gro. PR1—1C 8
Limbrick Rd. PR6—1J 25
Lime Chase. PR2—3G 3
Lime Clo. PR1—1E 10
Lime Gro. PR2—2D 6
Lime Gro. PR7—3G 25
Limes Av. PR2—3A 20
Limes, The. PR1—3B 8
Lincoln St. PR1—3B 8
(in two parts)
Lincoln Wlk. PR1—3B 8
Lindale Av. PR2—2K 5
Lindale Rd. PR2—7A 4
Linden Clo. PR5—4B 12
Linden Dri. PR5—4B 12
Linden Gro. PR2—1E 8
Linden Gro. PR6—4H 21
Lindle Av. PR4—3C 10
Lindle Clo. PR4—3C 10
Lindle Cres. PR4—3C 10
Lindle La. PR4—2C 10
Lindley St. PR5—5A 12
Lindsay Av. PR5—5K 15
Lindsay Dri. PR7—1E 24
Link Rd. PR5—7G 13
Linksfield. PR2—1G 7
Links Ga. PR2—1G 7
Links Rd. PR1—6F 7
Linnet St. PR1—2B 8
Linton Gro. PR1—7E 6
Linton St. PR1—2H 7
Liptrott Rd. PR7—3E 24
Lit. Banks Clo. PR5—7H 13
Lit. Carr La. PR7—3H & 3J 25
(in two parts)
Little Clo. PR1—2G 11
Liverpool Rd. PR4 & PR1
    —4A 10 to 6H 7
Livesey St. PR1—5B 8
Livesey St. PR7—7G 21
Lockhart Rd. PR1—2K 7
Lockside Rd. PR2—5D 6
Lodge Clo. PR5—4F 13
Lodge La. PR5—6H 11
Lodge St. PR1—4H & 4J 7
London St. PR1—5B 8
London Way. PR5—1C 12
Longbrook Av. PR5—3E 12
Long Acre. PR5—1G 17
Long Butts. PR1—3H 11
Long Clo. PR5—6C 14
Long Copse. PR7—6D 20
Long Croft Meadow. PR7
    —5F 21
Longfield. PR1—7F 7
Longfield. PR2—3K 3
Longfield Av. PR7—6C 24
Longley Clo. PR2—3K 3
Long Meadow. PR7—3E 24
Longmeanygate. PR5
    —4C 14 to 4F 15
Long Moss. PR5—6C 14
Long Moss La. PR4—7C 10
Longridge Rd. PR2—7F 5
Longsands La. PR2—6C 4
Longton By-Pass. PR4—7A 10
Longton St. PR6—7J 21
Longworth Av. PR7—6D 24
Longworth St. PR1—3C 8
Longworth St. PR7—2F 25

Lonsdale Clo. PR5—1J 19
Lonsdale Rd. PR1—3C 8
Lord's Av. PR5—6B 12
Lord's La. PR1—4J 11
Lord St. PR1—4A 8
Lord St. PR6—1H 25
(Chorley)
Lord St. PR6—5G 17
(Whittle-le-Woods)
Lord St. PR7—3E 22
Lord's Wlk. PR1—4A 8
Lorne St. PR7—1G 25
Lorraine Av. PR2—1J 7
Lorton Clo. PR2—5K 3
Lostock Ct. PR5—6B 12
Lostock La. PR5—6C 12
Lostock Sq. PR5—6B 12
Lostock View. PR5—6A 12
Lourdes Av. PR5—4A 12
Lovat Rd. PR1—2K 7
Low Croft. PR4—1F 3
Lowick Clo. PR5—1K 13
Lowndes St. PR1—2J 7
Lowood Gro. PR2—3B 6
Lowry Clo. PR5—6A 12
Lowther Cres. PR5—3F 15
Lowther Dri. PR5—4F 15
Lowther St. PR2—3G 7
Lowthian St. PR1—4K 7
Lowthorpe Cres. PR1—2B 8
Lowthorpe Pl. PR1—2B 8
Lowthorpe Rd. PR1—2B 8
Lucas Av. PR7—7B 20
Lucas La. PR6—2G 21
Lucerne Rd. PR2—7C 4
Ludwidge St. PR1—4B 8
Lulworth Av. PR2—2H 7
Lulworth Pl. PR5—3D 12
Lulworth Rd. PR2—7A 4
Lulworth St. PR5—3E 12
Lund St. PR1—4H 7
Lune Dri. PR5—4C 16
Lune St. PR1—5K 7
Lupton St. PR7—2G 25
Luton Rd. PR2—2D 6
Lutwidge Av. PR1—3C 8
Lydd Gro. PR7—1E 24
Lydgate. PR7—3E 24
Lydiate La. PR5—2A 16
Lydiate La. PR7—7D 18
Lydric Av. PR5—3K 13
Lyndale Av. PR5—3C 12
Lyndale Gro. PR5—3C 12
Lyndhurst Dri. PR2—2C 6
Lynn Pl. PR2—2D 8
Lynton Av. PR5—6A 16
Lynwood Av. PR2—1J 5
Lyons La. PR7 & PR6—1H 25
Lytham Clo. PR2—1H 7
Lytham Rd. PR2—1G 7
Lytham St. PR6—1J 25
Lythcoe Av. PR2—7G 3

McKenzie St. PR5—5F 13
Maddy St. PR1—4H 7
Mafeking Rd. PR2—2G 7
Magnolia Clo. PR2—5C 4
Magnolia Rd. PR1—2H 7
Main Sprit Weind. PR1—5A 8
Mainway Ct. PR5—5E 12
Maitland Clo. PR1—4C 8
Maitland St. PR1—4C 8
Malcolm St. PR1—3D 8
Malden St. PR5—5J 15
Maldon Pl. PR2—2D 8

Malham Pl. PR2—7E 4
Mallom Av. PR7—6C 20
Mall, The. PR2—2E 8
Malthouse Way. PR1—2H 11
Maltings, The. PR1—2H 11
Malton Dri. PR5—6A 12
Malvern Av. PR1—7B 8
Malvern Clo. PR5—5C 12
Malvern Ho. PR1—3J 11
Malvern Rd. PR1—6B 8
Manchester Rd. PR1—5A 8
Manning Rd. PR1—3E & 4E 8
Manor Av. PR1—1F 11
Manor Av. PR2—7B 4
Manor Ct. PR2—4F 3
Manor Gro. PR1—1E 10
Manor Ho. Clo. PR5—6D 14
Manor Ho. Cres. PR1—1B 8
Manor Ho. La. PR1—1B 8
Manor La. PR1—1E 10
Manor Pk. PR2—7C 4
Manor Rd. PR6—3F 17
Manston Gro. PR7—1E 24
Maplebank. PR2—3A 6
Maple Dri. PR5—4F 13
Maple Gro. PR1—1F 11
Maple Gro. PR2—2K 5
(Grimsargh)
Maple Gro. PR2—7G 5
(Ribbleton)
Maple Gro. PR6—4H 21
Maplewood Clo. PR5—6G 15
Marathon Pl. PR5—3E 14
Mardale Cres. PR5—7K 15
Mardale Rd. PR1—3G 9
Maresfield Rd. PR1—7H 7
Margaret Rd. PR1—1J 11
Margate Rd. PR2—7E 2
Margate St. PR1—4A 8
Marilyn Av. PR5—5B 12
Marina Clo. PR5—4A 12
Marina Dri. PR2—4J 3
Marina Dri. PR5—4A 12
Marina Gro. PR5—4A 12
Mariners Way. PR2—4E 6
Mark Clo. PR1—5A 8
Market Pl. PR1—5A 8
Market Pl. PR7—7G 21
Market St. PR1—4K 7
Market St. PR7—7G 21
Market St. W. PR1—4K 7
Markham St. PR2—3G 7
Markland St. PR1—5J 7
Mark's Av. PR5—1G 15
Marl Av. PR1—1F 11
Marlborough Dri. PR2—4H 3
Marlborough Dri. PR5—1D 12
Marlborough St. PR6—6J 21
Marl Croft. PR1—3H 11
Marlfield Clo. PR6—6D 2
Marl Hill Cres. PR2—2G 9
Marron Clo. PR5—6G 15
Marsden Clo. PR7—1D 22
Marsett Pl. PR2—6E 4
Marshall Gro. PR2—7E 2
Marshall's Brow. PR1—2J 11
Marshall's Clo. PR1—1J 11
Marsh La. PR1—5H to 4K 7
(in three parts)
Marsh Way. PR1—3G 11
Marston Clo. PR2—3K 3
Marston Moor. PR2—4G 3
Martindales, The. PR6—3E 16
Martinfield. PR2—3K 3
Martin Field Rd. PR1—3H 11
Martins Av. PR7—6J 25
Marton Rd. PR2—4D 6
Marybank Clo. PR2—5C 4
Masefield Pl. PR5—3D 12
Masonfield. PR5—1F 17
Mason Ho. Cres. PR2—6E 2
Mason St. PR6—5J 21
Masonwood. PR2—5A 4
Matlock Pl. PR2—6E 2
Matterdale Rd. PR5—7K 15

Maudland Bank. PR1—4J 7
Maudland Rd. PR1—4J 7
Maud St. PR7—2F 25
Maureen Av. PR5—5B 12
Mavis Dri. PR7—7C 24
Mayfield Av. PR2—7F 3
Mayfield Av. PR5—5C 12
Mayfield Rd. PR2—3F 7
Mayfield Rd. PR5—7J 15
Mayfield Rd. PR6—6H 21
Mayflower Av. PR1—2E 10
Maynard St. PR2 & PR1—2H 7
Maypark. PR5—1E 16
Mead Av. PR5—6K 15
Meadow Bank. PR1—2G 11
Meadow Bank. PR5—2F 17
Meadow Ct. PR1—6J 7
Meadowcroft. PR7—4K 19
Meadowcroft Rd. PR5—1F 15
Meadowfield. PR1—3J 11
Meadowfield. PR2—3K 3
Meadowlands. PR7—4B 24
Meadow La. PR5—2F 17
Meadowside Dri. PR5—4K 13
Meadows, The. PR5—5D 14
Meadows, The. PR7—6G 23
Meadow St. PR1—4A 8
Meadow St. PR5—5J 15
Meadow Way. PR7—7B 24
Meads Rd. PR2—3F 7
Meadway. PR1—7E 6
Meadway. PR6—3F 17
Mealhouse La. PR7—7G 21
Meanygate. PR5—5E 12
Mearley Rd. PR2—7E 4
Meath Rd. PR1—6H 7
Medway. PR2—5K 3
Medway Clo. PR5—4B 12
Melba Rd. PR2—1E 8
Melbert Av. PR2—1G 7
Melbourne St. PR1—4K 7
Mellings Fold. PR1—6C 8
Melling St. PR1—4K 7
Melling's Yd. PR1—5K 7
Mellor Pl. PR1—5B 8
Mellor Rd. PR5—4F 15
Melrose Av. PR2—6B 4
Melrose Way. PR7—2H 25
Melton Pl. PR5—5K 15
Menai Dri. PR2—4H 3
Mendip Rd. PR5—5B 16
Mercer Rd. PR5—4A 12
Mercer St. PR1—4C 8
Mere Clo. PR3—1G 3
Merefield. PR7—6E 20
Mere Fold. PR7—5B 24
Merrick Av. PR1—4F 9
Mersey St. PR1—4G 7
Merton Av. PR2—5K 3
Merton Gro. PR6—4K 21
Mete St. PR1—4D 8
Methuen Av. PR2—5J 3
Mickleden Av. PR2—4K 3
Middlefield. PR5—6C 14
Middleforth Grn. PR1—1J 11
Midge Hall La. PR5—1A 14
Midgery La. PR3 & PR2—3B 4
Miles St. PR1—2K 7
Miles Wlk. PR1—2J 7
Millbank. PR2—1G 7
Millbrook Way. PR1—3F 11
Millcroft. PR2—7H 3
Millcroft. PR7—5E 20
Miller Field. PR2—1C 6
Miller La. PR4—6C 2
Miller Rd. PR1 & PR2
—3D 8 to 2F 9
Miller's La. PR5—3D 14
Miller St. PR1—4C 8
Millfield Rd. PR7—6F 21
Mill Fold. PR1—3K 7
Millgate. PR2—1H 7
Millgate. PR7—7B 20
Millhaven. PR2—1H 7
Mill Hill. PR1—4J 7

Mill La. PR2—7G 3
Mill La. PR5—3G 15
(Farington Moss)
Mill La. PR5—6F 15
(Leyland)
Mill La. PR5—7D 8
(Walton-le-Dale)
Mill La. PR6—5G 17
Mill La. PR7—6J 23
(Charnock Richard)
Mill La. PR7—6C 24
(Coppull)
Mill La. PR7—3E 22
(Eccleston)
Mill La. PR7—6J & 7J 19
(Euxton, in two parts)
Mill Row. PR1—2K 11
Mill St. PR1—4H 7
Mill St. PR5—3K 15
(Farington)
Mill St. PR5—6F 15
(Leyland)
Mill St. PR6—7K 17
Mill St. PR7—7C 24
Millwood Glade. PR7—6F 21
Millwood Rd. PR5—2B 12
Milner St. PR1—2K 7
Milton Clo. PR5—3D 12
Milton Ct. PR7—7C 24
Milton Rd. PR7—7C 24
Milton Ter. PR6—5H 21
Mimosa Rd. PR2—2E 8
Mitton Dri. PR2—1G 9
Moira Cres. PR2—7F 5
Mona Pl. PR1—4J 7
Monks Wlk. PR1—6G 7
Montcliffe Rd. PR6—6J 21
Montgomery St. PR5—5F 13
Montjolly St. PR1—5C 8
Montrose Clo. PR6—2J 25
Moody La. L40—7A 22
Moon St. PR5—5E 12
Moor Av. PR1—2D 10
Moorbrook St. PR1—3J 7
Moorcroft. PR3—1F 3
Moorcroft Cres. PR2—1D 8
Moore St. PR1—5C 8
Moor Field. PR2—1E 8
Moorfield Clo. PR2—3J 3
Moorfield Dri. PR2—1E 8
Moorfield Rd. PR5—6E 14
Moorfields. PR6—6J 21
Moorfields Av. PR2—3J 3
Moorgate. PR2—6K 3
Moor Hall St. PR1—2J 7
Moorhey Cres. PR1—7F 7
Moorhey Cres. PR5—5G 13
Moorhey Dri. PR1—7F 7
Moorland Av. PR2—6D 4
Moorland Cres. PR2—6D 4
Moorland Ga. PR6—2K 25
Moorlands. PR1—1J 7
Moor La. PR1—4K 7
Moor La. PR4—4B 10
Moor Pk. Av. PR1—2K 7
Moor Rd. PR5—4A 18
Moor Rd. PR7—3E 24
Moorside Av. PR2—1F 9
Morland Av. PR5—6A 12
Mornington Rd. PR1—7F 7
(Penwortham)
Mornington Rd. PR1—3F 9
(Preston)
Morris Ct. PR2—2D 8
Morris Cres. PR2—2D 8
Morrison St. PR6—5H 21
Morris Rd. PR2—2D 8
Morris Rd. PR6—6J 21
Mosley St. PR1—4C 8
Mosley St. PR5—5J 15
Moss Acre Rd. PR1—2J 11
Moss Av. PR2—2E 6
(in two parts)
Moss Bri. Pk. PR5—5C 12
Moss Clo. PR6—7J 21

Mossdale Av. PR2—7D 4
Mossfield Clo. PR5—5B 12
Mossfield Rd. PR6—7J 21
Moss Ho. Rd. PR4—1F 3
Moss La. PR1—5J 11
Moss La. PR4—5B 10
Moss La. PR5—6A 14
(Cocker Bar)
Moss La. PR5—1E 14
(Farington Moss)
Moss La. PR5—4K 15
(Leyland)
Moss La. PR5—5B 12
(Lostock Hall)
Moss La. PR5—1B 18
(Ulnes Walton)
Moss La. PR6—2G 21
(in three parts)
Moss La. PR7—7C 24
Moss Side Way. PR5—7D 14
Moss St. PR1—4J 7
Moss St. PR5—5B 12
Moss Ter. PR6—2J 21
Mossway. PR4—7D 10
Mounsey Rd. PR5—5F 13
Mountain Rd. PR7—7C 24
Mountbatten Rd. PR7—2E 24
Mt. Pleasant. PR1—4K 7
Mt. Pleasant. PR6—6G 17
Mount St. PR1—5K 7
Muirfield. PR1—6E 6
Muirfield Clo. PR2—5F 3
Mulberry Av. PR1—2E 10
Mulgrave Av. PR2—3E 6
Muncaster Rd. PR1—2K 7
Munro Cres. PR2—1E 8
Murdock Av. PR2—2H 7
Murray Av. PR5—1G 15
Murray St. PR1—3J 7
Murray St. PR5—5K 15
Mythop Pl. PR2—3D 6

Nab Rd. PR6—6J 21
Naptha La. PR4—6G 11
Nares St. PR2—3G 7
Narrow La. PR5—4B 14
Nateby Pl. PR2—3D 6
Navigation Way. PR2—4D 6
Neargates. PR7—5B 24
Nell La. PR5—2B 16
Nelson Av. PR5—5K 15
Nelson Cres. PR2—2B 6
Nelson Dri. PR2—2B 6
Nelson Rd. PR7—1G 25
Nelson St. PR5—5E 12
Nelson Way. PR2—5C 6
Nene Clo. PR5—7K 15
Neston St. PR1—4E 8
Netherley Rd. PR7—7C 24
Nevett St. PR1—4D 8
Newark Pl. PR2—2C 6
(Ashton-on-Ribble)
Newark Pl. PR2—3H 3
(Fulwood)
New Brook Ho. PR1—4C 8
Newbury Clo. PR2—3G 3
Newbury Grn. PR2—3G 3
Newby Dri. PR5—4C 16
Newby Pl. PR2—7D 4
(in two parts)
New Cock Yd. PR1—5K 7
Newfield Rd. PR5—6G 13
Newgate. PR2—7J 3
Newgate La. PR4—6G 11
New Hall La. PR1—4B 8
Newlands. PR7—2E 22
Newlands Av. PR1—1E 10
New La. PR1—2J 11
New La. PR7—5C 18
New Links Av. PR2—5E 2
Newlyn Pl. PR2—6D 2
New Market St. PR1—4C 16
New Mill St. PR7—2E 22
New Moss La. PR6—2G 21

New Pastures. PR5—5C 12
New Rd. PR5—4B 12
New Rd. PR7—6D 24
New Rough Hey. PR2—5D 2
Newsham Hall La. PR4—1D 2
Newsham La. PR4—1F 3
Newsham St. PR2—3H 7
Newsome St. PR5—5J 15
New St. PR7—2E 22
Newton Av. PR1—4G 9
Newton Clo. PR5—6D 14
Newton Ct. PR2—3F 7
Newton Rd. PR2—2F 7
Newton St. PR1—4B 8
(in two parts)
Nichol St. PR7—6G 21
Nimes St. PR1—4D 8
Nine Elms. PR2—5G 3
Nixon La. PR5—6B 14
Noel Sq. PR2—3E 8
Nook Cres. PR2—2J 5
Nookfield. PR5—5C 14
Nook Glade. PR2—2J 5
Nooklands. PR2—7J 3
Nook La. L40—3A 22
Nook La. PR5—6D 12
Noor St. PR1—3A 8
Norbreck Dri. PR2—3C 6
Norcross Pl. PR2—3C 6
Norfolk Clo. PR5—7G 15
Norfolk Rd. PR1—3A 8
Norfolk Rd. PR5—1D 12
Normandy Rd. PR4—1F 3
Norris St. PR1—2H 7
Norris St. PR1—1H 7
Norris St. PR7—2E 25
Northbrook Rd. PR5
(in two parts)   —4G & 5G 15
N. Cliff St. PR1—6J 7
Northcote Rd. PR1—5H 7
Northenden Rd. PR7—7C 24
Northgate. PR5—4K 15
Northgate Dri. PR6—5J 21
North Gro. PR5—5C 12
Northlands. PR2—5J 3
Northlands. PR5—7E 14
Northleach Av. PR1—3K 11
N. Ribble St. PR5—6C 8
North Rd. PR1—3K 7
Northside. PR7—4A 20
North St. PR1—4K 7
North St. PR7—5H 21
N. Syke Av. PR2—3A 6
North Ter. PR7—3B 20
Northumberland St. PR7
—1H 25
North Vale. PR6—7K 25
North View. PR5—6H 15
Northway. PR2—4H 3
Northway. PR3—1G 3
Norwich Pl. PR1—5A 8
Nottingham Rd. PR1—3A 8
Nursery Clo. PR5—6H 15
Nursery Clo. PR7—4C 24
Nursery La. PR5—5C 10
Nutter Rd. PR1—5J 7

Oak Av. PR1—2F 11
Oak Av. PR7—4B 20
Oak Croft. PR6—4F 17
Oakenhead St. PR1—3E 8
Oakfield. PR2—3F 7
(Ashton-on-Ribble)
Oakfield. PR2—4K 3
(Fulwood)
Oakfield Dri. PR5—6E 14
Oak Gro. PR4—7E 10
Oakham Ct. PR1—5A 8
Oakland Glen Caravan Pk. PR5
—2A 12
Oaklands Dri. PR1—1E 10
Oakland St. PR5—4E 12
Oakmere. PR6—3G 17
Oakridge Clo. PR2—4K 3

Oakshott Pl. PR5—6H 13
Oaks, The. PR5—2B 12
Oaks, The. PR7—7F 25
Oak St. PR1—5A 8
Oaktree Av. PR2—7E 2
Oak Tree Av. PR5—2B 16
Oak View. PR5—4G 15
Oakwood Av. PR5—1C 12
Oakwood Dri. PR2—3H 3
Oakwood Rd. PR7—2F 25
(Chorley)
Oakwood Rd. PR7—6D 24
(Coppull)
Oakwood View. PR7—4F 25
Oakworth Av. PR2—6F 5
Oban Ct. PR2—2K 5
Oban Cres. PR1—1D 8
Old Brown La. PR5—2G 13
Old Dawber's La. PR7—6K 19
Old Dock Yd. PR1—5A 8
Oldfield. PR1—3H 11
Oldfield Rd. PR5—6G 13
Old Hall Clo. PR5—5E 12
Old Hall Dri. PR5—5E 12
Old Hall La. PR7—2K 23
Old Lancaster La. PR1—3H 7
Old Mill Ter. PR6—6J 21
Old Pope La. PR4—5F 11
Old School Clo. PR5—6C 14
Old School La. PR5—7C 12
Old School La. PR7—4B 20
(in two parts)
Old Station Clo. PR2—2K 5
Old Tram Rd. PR1—1A & 2B 12
Old Tram Rd. PR5
(in two parts)—5E 12 & 6F 13
Old Vicarage. PR1—4A 8
Olivers Way. PR2—3A 4
Orchard Av. PR4—6E 10
Orchard Croft. PR5—5A 12
Orchard St. PR1—4K 7
Orchard St. PR5—5K 15
Orchard, The. PR4—2C 2
Ord Rd. PR2—2G 7
Ormskirk Rd. PR1—4A 8
Orrell Clo. PR5—5F 15
Orrest Rd. PR1—3G 9
Osborne Rd. PR5—2D 12
Osborne St. PR1—5J 7
Oswald Rd. PR2—3G 7
Otters Clo. PR2—2F 9
Otway St. PR1—2J 7
Outram Way. PR5—5E 12
Overton Rd. PR2—4C 6
Owens St. PR6—1J 25
Owen St. PR1—4B 8
Owtram St. PR1—4C 8
Oxford Rd. PR2—7H 3
Oxford Rd. PR5—5F 13
Oxford St. PR1—5A 8
Oxford St. PR7—1G 25
Oxhey Av. PR2—2A 6
Oxheys Ind. Est. PR1—2H 7
Oxheys St. PR1—2H 7
Oxley Rd. PR1—3D 8
(in two parts)

Paddock, The. PR1—3J 11
Paddock, The. PR2—5A 4
Padway. PR1—3H 11
Pages Ct. PR5—6B 12
Paley Rd. PR1—5H 7
Pall Mall. PR1—2G 25
Paplar Av. PR7—3A 20
Paradise La. PR5—5D 14
Paradise St. PR6—4K 21
Park Av. PR1—2B 8
Park Av. PR4—4C 10
Park Av. PR7—5B 20
Park Clo. PR1—1H 11
Park Dri. PR2—3B 6
Parker La. PR4—7G 11
Parker St. PR2—2H 7
Parker St. PR7—6G 21

Parkfield Av. PR2—2F 7
Parkfield Clo. PR2—3A 6
Parkfield Clo. PR5—6E 14
Parkfield Cres. PR2—4A 6
Parkfield Dri. PR2—4A 6
Parkgate Dri. PR5—7G 15
Park Hall Rd. PR7—4G 23
Parklands Av. PR1—1E 10
Parklands Clo. PR1—1E 10
Parklands Dri. PR2—3J 3
Parklands Gro. PR2—3J 3
Park La. PR1—2J 11
Park Mill Pl. PR1—3A 8
Park Pl. PR5—1E 12
Park Rd. PR1—1H 11
(Penwortham)
Park Rd. PR1—4A 8
(Preston)
Park Rd. PR2—7A 4
Park Rd. PR5—7J 15
Park Rd. PR7—7G 21
(Chorley)
Park Rd. PR7—7C 24
(Coppull)
Parkside. PR1—1B 8
Parkside. PR2—2B 6
Parkside Av. PR7—7G 21
Parkside Dri. PR6—1F 21
(in two parts)
Parkstone Rd. PR3—1G 3
Park St. PR7—6G 21
Parkthorn Rd. PR2—4A 6
Park View. PR1—1H 11
Park View Av. PR2—2F 7
Park Wlk. PR2—1A 8
Park Way. PR1—1H 11
Parlick Rd. PR2—2G 9
Parr Cottage Clo. PR7—1E 22
Parr La. PR7—1E 22
Parrock Clo. PR1—2J 11
Parsons Brow. PR7—1G 25
Pasture Field Clo. PR5—5E 14
Patten St. PR1—4K 7
Pavillions, The. PR2—5G 7
Peacock Hall Rd. PR5—7F 15
Pearfield. PR5—4J 15
Pear Tree Av. PR7—5D 24
Pear Tree Clo. PR5—3E 12
Pear Tree Cres. PR5—3E 12
Pear Tree La. PR7—4C 20
Pear Tree Rd. PR6—3F 17
Pear Tree St. PR5—3E 12
Pechell St. PR2—3G 7
Pedder's Gro. PR2—4E 6
Pedder's La. PR2—4E 6
Pedder St. PR2—4H 7
Pedder's Way. PR2—4E 6
Peel Hall St. PR1—3B 8
(in two parts)
Peel St. PR2—4J 7
Peel St. PR7—1G 25
Pembroke Pl. PR1—5A 8
Pembroke Pl. PR5—6J 15
Pembroke Pl. PR7—2F 25
Pembury Av. PR1—2K 11
Pendle Rd. PR5—5B 16
Penguin St. PR1—2B 8
Pennine Av. PR7—6B 20
Pennine Rd. PR6—7J 21
Pennines, The. PR2—4A 4
Penny St. PR1—4A 8
Penwortham Ct. PR1—1H 11
Penwortham Hall Gdns. PR1
—2J 11
Penwortham Way. PR1 & PR4
—3F 11
Pen-y-Ghent Way. PR5—4A 16
Percy St. PR1—4A 8
Percy St. PR7—1H 25
Peterfield. PR1—3H 11
Peter St. PR7—7G 21
Pickerings, The. PR5—5C 12
Pikestone Ct. PR6—1J 25
Pilling Clo. PR7—2H 25
Pilling La. PR7—3G 25

Pincock Brow. PR7—7A 20
Pincock St. PR7—7A 20
Pine Clo. PR2—7F 5
Pine Gro. PR6—4H 21
Pines Clo. PR5—2G 17
Pines, The. PR5—6J 15
Pine Walks. PR2—3A 6
Pineway. PR2—7G 3
Pinewood Av. PR3—1G 3
Pinewood Cres. PR5—6G 15
Pinfold St. PR1—4D 8
Pingle Croft. PR6—4E 16
Pippin St. PR6—2J 17
Pitman Way. PR2—3B 4
Pitt St. PR1—5J 7
Plant St. PR2—3G 7
Pleasant View. PR7—6D 24
Plevna Rd. PR1—4C 8
Plock Grn. PR7—3G 25
Plover St. PR1—2B 8
Plumpton Field. PR4—1C 2
Plumpton La. PR4—2B 2
Plumpton Rd. PR2—2G 7
Plungington Rd. PR2 & PR1
—1H 7
Plymouth Gro. PR6—7J 21
Polefield. PR2—4J 3
Pole St. PR1—4A 8
Pollard St. PR1—4J 7
Poole Rd. PR2—7A 4
Pool Ho. La. PR2—6D 2
Pope La. PR2—2F 9 to 7J 5
Pope La. PR4 & PR1
—6F to 2H 11
Pope Wlk. PR1—2H 11
Poplar Av. PR5—4F 13
Poplar Clo. PR5—4F 13
Poplar Dri. PR1—7G 7
Poplar Gro. PR2—7G 5
Poplar Gro. PR5—4F 13
Poplar St. PR7—2H 25
Porter Pl. PR1—6A 8
Porter St. PR1—3B 8
Portland St. PR1—5H 7
Portland St. PR7—7H 21
Portman St. PR1—4B 8
Portree Clo. PR2—6C 4
Portsmouth Dri. PR6—7J 21
Port Way. PR2—4G 7
Potter La. PR5—6J 9
(Higher Walton)
Potter La. PR5—3K 9
(Samlesbury)
Poulton Cres. PR5—2K 13
Poulton St. PR2—3C 8
Powis Rd. PR2—4E 6
Poynter St. PR1—3C 8
Preesall Clo. PR2—3C 6
Preesall Rd. PR2—3C 6
Preston New Rd. PR5—3H 9
Preston Rd. PR2—3J 5
Preston Rd. PR5 & PR6
—7G 13 to 5G 21
(Clayton Brook)
Preston Rd. PR5—4K 15
(Leyland)
Preston Rd. PR7—5K 23
(Charnock Richard)
Preston Rd. PR7—7A 24
(Coppull)
Preston St. PR7—6H 21
Pretoria St. PR5—5E 12
Primrose Gro. PR1—1C 8
Primrose Hill. PR1—5B 8
Primrose Hill Rd. PR7—3K 19
Primrose La. PR1—1C 8
Primrose Rd. PR1—1C 8
Primrose St. PR6—7H 21
Princes Dri. PR2—5J 3
Princes Reach. PR2—5E 6
Princes Rd. PR1—6F 7
Prince's Rd. PR5—7E 8
Princess Clo. PR1—6F 7
Princess St. PR1—5B 8

Princess St. PR5—5F 13
(Bamber Bridge)
Princess St. PR5—5K 15
(Leyland)
Princess St. PR5—6B 12
(Lostock Hall)
Princess St. PR7—2H 25
Princess Way. PR7—5B 12
Prince's Way. PR7—5C 20
Prior's Oak Cottages. PR1
—7G 7
Priory Clo. PR1—6G 7
Priory Clo. PR5—4A 16
Priory Cres. PR1—6G 7
Priory La. PR1—7F 7
Priory St. PR2—4H 7
Progress St. PR6—7J 21
Prospect Av. PR5—5B 12
Prospect Pl. PR1—1J 11
Prospect Pl. PR2—3F 7
Prospect View. PR5—6B 12
Pump Ho. La. PR5—1B 18
Pump St. PR1—4A 8

Quarry Rd. PR6—2J 25
Queenscourt Av. PR1—3J 11
Queen's Dri. PR2—5H 3
Queensgate. PR7—1F 25
Queen's Gro. PR7—7G 21
Queen's Rd. PR2—1H 7
Queen's Rd. PR5—7E 8
Queen's Rd. PR7—7F 21
Queen St. PR1—5B 8
Queen St. PR5—6B 12
Queen St. PR7—2H 25
Queensway. PR1—6F 7
Queens Way. PR2—2D 6
Queensway. PR5—4E 12
(Bamber Bridge)
Queensway. PR5—7G 15
(Leyland)
Queensway. PR7—5C 20
Queensway Clo. PR1—6F 7
Quin St. PR5—5J 15

Radburn Brow. PR6—3F 17
Radburn Clo. PR6—3F 17
Radnor St. PR1—4J 7
Raglan St. PR2—2H 7
Raikes Rd. PR1—3C 8
Railway Rd. PR6—6H 21
Railway St. PR5—4K 15
Railway St. PR7—1H 25
Raleigh Rd. PR2—5J 3
Ramsey Av. PR1—1D 8
Ranaldsway. PR5—6E 14
Ranglet Rd. PR5—6H 13
Rangletts Av. PR7—2G 25
Ranglit Av. PR2—3A 6
Ratten La. PR4—2A 10
Ravenhill Dri. PR7—6G 21
Ravensthorpe. PR7—6E 20
Raven St. PR1—2C 8
Rawcliffe Dri. PR2—4C 6
Rawcliffe Rd. PR7—1G 25
Rawlinson La. PR7 & PR6
—6J 25
Rawstorne Rd. PR1—7F 7
Rectory Clo. PR7—7G 21
Red Bank. PR7—3H 25
Redcar Av. PR2—7E 2
Red Cross St. PR1—5J 7
Redhill. PR4—4A 10
Redhill Gro. PR6—4J 21
Red Ho. La. PR7—2D 22
Red La. PR7—1F 23
Redmayne St. PR1—4D 8
Red Scar Ind. Est. PR2—6H 5
Redwood Av. PR5—5E 12
Reedfield. PR5—2G 17
Reedfield St. PR5—7G 13
Regency Av. PR5—6D 12
Regent Ct. PR2—6J 3

Regent Dri. PR2—7H 3
Regent Gro. PR2—6J 3
Regent Pk. PR2—6J 3
Regent Rd. PR5—5J 15
  (Leyland)
Regent Rd. PR5—1D 12
  (Walton-le-Dale)
Regent Rd. PR7—1F 25
Regent St. PR1—6K 7
Regent St. PR7—7C 24
Regentsway. PR5—4E 12
Regents Way. PR7—5B 20
Reigate. PR6—4K 21
Reiver Rd. PR5—3E 14
Renshaw Dri. PR5—3E 12
Rhoden Rd. PR5—5E 14
Rhodesway. PR5—3K 13
Ribble Bank. PR1—6F 7
Ribble Bank St. PR1—5J 7
Ribble Clo. PR1—1J 11
  (Penwortham)
Ribble Clo. PR1—7J 7
  (Preston)
Ribble Ct. PR2—3G 7
Ribble Cres. PR5—6C 8
Ribble Rd. PR5—6F 15
Ribblesdale Dri. PR2—3J 5
Ribblesdale Pl. PR1—6K 7
Ribblesdale Pl. PR7—1F 25
Ribble St. PR1—5J 7
Ribbleton Av. PR1 & PR2
            —2D 8 to 1F 9
Ribbleton Hall Cres. PR2—1F 9
Ribbleton Hall Dri. PR2—1F 9
Ribbleton La. PR1—4B 8
Ribbleton Pl. PR1—4B 8
Ribbleton St. PR1—4B 8
Ribby Pl. PR2—3D 6
Richmond Rd. PR6—2J 25
Richmond Rd. PR7—1E 22
Richmond St. PR1—5B 8
Ridgeford Gdns. PR2—6H 3
Ridgemont. PR2—5G 3
Ridge Rd. PR6—1J 25
Ridgeway. PR1—1J 11
Riding St. PR1—3K 7
Ridley Rd. PR2—2G 7
Rigby St. PR1—3C 8
Ring Way. PR1—4K 7
Ringway. PR7—1E 24
Ringwood Rd. PR1—2C 8
Ripon St. PR1—2H 7
Ripon Ter. PR1—3F 9
River Heights. PR5—5C 12
River Pde. PR1—6H 7
Riversedge Rd. PR5—6E 14
Riverside. PR1—7J 7
  (Penwortham)
Riverside. PR1—7J 7
  (Preston)
Riverside. PR5—6E 12
Riverside Av. PR5—2G 15
Riverside Clo. PR5—2G 15
Riverside Ter. PR5—2G 15
River St. PR1—5J 7
Riversway. PR2—4A 6
Riversway Bus. Village. PR2
            —4F 7
Riverway Clo. PR5—5D 12
Rivington Rd. PR6—6J 21
Roberts St. PR7—1G 25
Robin Clo. PR5—5B 24
Robin Hey. PR5—5D 14
Robinson St. PR2—1H 7
Robin St. PR1—3D 8
Rock Villa Rd. PR6—6G 17
Rodney St. PR1—4J 7
Roebuck St. PR2—2G 7
Roe Hey Dri. PR7—6D 24
Roman Rd. PR1—5B 8
Roman Way. PR2—5J 5
Roman Way Ind. Est. PR2—5J 5
Romford Rd. PR1—2C 8
Ronaldsway. PR1—1D 8

Rookery Clo. PR1—3K 11
Rookery Clo. PR7—2E 24
Rookery Dri. PR1—3K 11
Rook St. PR1—2B 8
Rookwood. PR7—2D 22
Rookwood Av. PR7—5G 21
Roseacre Pl. PR2—3C 6
Rose Av. PR2—1G 7
Rosebank. PR2—3A 6
Rose Fold. PR1—1H 11
Rose Hill. PR7—3A 20
Rose La. PR1—1C 8
Rosemary Ct. PR1—3G 11
Rosemeade Av. PR5—5B 12
Rose St. PR1—5A 8
Rose St. PR5—3K 15
Rose Ter. PR2—3F 7
Roseway. PR2—3E 6
Rosewood Av. PR5—2J 13
Rosewood Dri. PR5—2H 13
Roshaw. PR2—2K 5
Rosklyn Rd. PR6—1J 25
Rossall Clo. PR5—1K 13
Rossall Dri. PR2—7G 3
Rossall Rd. PR2—7G 3
Rossall Rd. PR6—6J 21
Rossall St. PR2—3G 7
Rostrevor Clo. PR5—5D 14
Rotherwick Av. PR7—1F 25
Rothwell Ct. PR5—4J 15
Rothwell Cres. PR2—7F 5
Rough Hey Rd. PR2—4H 5
Round Acre. PR1—4A 12
Round Meadow. PR5—5E 14
Roundway Down. PR2—4G 3
Rowan Av. PR2—7G 5
Rowan Clo. PR1—2F 11
Rowan Croft. PR6—5E 16
Rowan Gro. PR6—4G 21
Rowberrow Clo. PR2—5D 4
Rowton Heath. PR2—4H 3
Royal Av. PR2—5J 3
Royal Av. PR5—7G 15
Royalty Av. PR4—5E 10
Royalty La. PR4—5D 10
Royle Rd. PR7—7F 21
Rufus St. PR1—2C 8
Rundle Rd. PR1—2H 7
Runshaw Hall La. PR7—2J 19
Runshaw La. PR7
            —5F 19 to 3A 20
Rushey Hey. PR5—5A 12
Ruskin Av. PR5—5J 15
Ruskin St. PR1—6B 8
Rusland Dri. PR5—1K 13
Russell Av. PR1—4G 9
Russell Av. PR5—6A 16
Russell Sq. PR6—6H 21
Russell Sq. W. PR6—6H 21
Rutland Av. PR5—2D 12
Rutland St. PR1—4C 8
Rydal Av. PR1—2G 11
Rydal Av. PR5—4D 12
Rydal Clo. PR2—7C 4
Rydal Pl. PR7—2F 25
Rydal Rd. PR1—2D 8
Ryddingwood. PR1—6F 7
Ryden Av. PR5—5A 16
Ryefield. PR6—7K 17
Ryefield Av. PR1—3H 11
Ryelands Cres. PR2—4C 6
Rye St. PR1—3A 8
Rylands Rd. PR7—1F 25

Sackville St. PR6—1J 25
Sagar St. PR7—2E 22
Sage Ct. PR1—3G 11
Sage La. PR1—1B 8
St Aiden's Rd. PR5—3E 12
St Alban's Pl. PR7—3H 25
St Ambrose Ter. PR5—4K 15
St Andrew's Av. PR2—2E 6
St Andrew's Clo. PR5—7J 15
St Andrew's Rd. PR1—2A 8

St Andrews Way. PR5—6J 15
St Anne's Rd. PR5—3A 16
St Anne's Rd. PR6—1J 25
St Anne's St. PR1—2A 8
St Anthony's Clo. PR2—7G 3
St Anthony's Cres. PR2—7G 3
St Anthony's Dri. PR2—7G 3
St Anthony's Rd. PR1—2A 8
St Austin's Pl. PR1—5B 8
St Austin's Rd. PR1—5A 8
St Barnabas Pl. PR1—3A 8
St Catherines Clo. PR5—4A 16
St Catherine's Dri. PR2—7G 3
St Chad's Rd. PR1—3C 8
St Christine's Av. PR5—2A 16
St Christopher's Rd. PR1—2A 8
St Clare's Av. PR2—5A 4
St Clements Av. PR5—3A 16
St Cuthbert's Clo. PR2—1H 7
St Cuthbert's Rd. PR1—2A 8
St Cuthbert's Rd. PR5—4A 12
St David's Rd. PR1—2A 8
St David's Rd. PR5—4A 16
St Francis Clo. PR2—4A 4
St George's Cen. PR1—5K 7
St George's Rd. PR1—2K 7
St George's St. PR1—5K 7
St Gerrard's Rd. PR5—4A 12
St Gregory Rd. PR1—2B 8
St Gregory's Pl. PR7—3G 25
St Helen's Rd. PR6—5G 17
St Hilda's Clo. PR7—4G 25
St Ignatius Pl. PR1—4A 8
St Ignatius Sq. PR1—4A 8
St Ives Cres. PR2—7E 2
St James Clo. PR5—5B 12
St James St. PR5—5B 12
St James Lodge. PR5—6D 14
St James's Gdns. PR5—6C 14
St James's Pl. PR6—1J 25
St James's Rd. PR1—2K 7
St James's St. PR6—1J 25
St John's Cen. PR1—4A 8
  (off Lancaster Rd.)
St John's Clo. PR6—7F 17
St John's Grn. PR5—5G 15
St John's Pl. PR1—5A 8
St John's Rd. PR5—7D 8
St Joseph's Ter. PR1—3C 8
St Jude's Av. PR5—4D 12
  (Bamber Bridge)
St Judes Av. PR5—2A 16
  (Farington)
St Leonards Clo. PR2—1E 6
  (off Margate Rd.)
St Luke's Pl. PR1—3C 8
St Margaret's Rd. PR5—4A 16
St Mark's Pl. E. PR1—4H 7
St Mark's Pl. W. PR1—4H 7
St Mark's Rd. PR1—4H 7
St Marlowes Av. PR5—3A 16
St Martin's Rd. PR1—2A 8
St Mary's Av. PR5—4D 12
St Mary's Clo. PR1—4C 8
St Mary's Clo. PR5—4D 12
St Mary's Ct. PR1—4B 8
St Mary's Ga. PR7—4A 20
St Mary's Rd. PR5—4E 12
St Mary's St. PR1—4B 8
St Mary's St. N. PR1—4B 8
St Mary's Wlk. PR7—7G 21
St Michael's Clo. PR7—6F 20
St Michael's Rd. PR1—2A 8
St Michael's Rd. PR5—3A 16
St Oswald's Clo. PR1—2C 8
St Patrick's Pl. PR5—1E 12
St Paul's Av. PR1—3A 8
St Pauls Clo. PR5—6K 11
St Paul's Rd. PR1—2A 8
St Paul's Sq. PR1—4A 8
St Peter's Sq. PR1—4J 7
St Peter's St. PR1—4K 7
St Peter's St. PR6—6J 21
St Philip's Rd. PR1—2A 8
St Saviour's Clo. PR5—6F 13

St Stephen's Rd. PR1—2A 8
St Theresa's Dri. PR2—7G 3
St Thomas' Pl. PR1—3K 7
St Thomas Rd. PR1—2K 7
St Thomas's Rd. PR7—7G 21
St Thomas St. PR1—3K 7
St Vincent's Rd. PR2—6J 3
St Walburge Av. PR2—4J 7
St Walburge's Gdns PR2—4H 7
St Wilfrid St. PR1—5K 7
Salisbury Rd. PR1—5H 7
Salisbury St. PR1—3D 8
Salisbury St. PR7—1H 25
Salmon St. PR1—5C 8
Salter St. PR1—3K 7
Salt Pit La. L40—4B 22
Salwick Pl. PR2—3C 6
Samuel St. PR1—4D 8
Sanderson La. PR7—7C 22
Sandfield St. PR5—5K 7
Sandgate. PR7—3H 25
Sandham St. PR6—7H 21
Sandown Ct. PR1—5A 8
Sandridge Av. PR7—1F 25
Sandringham Av. PR5—3A 16
Sandringham Pk. Dri. PR4
            —5E 10
Sandringham Rd. PR5—2D 12
Sandringham Rd. PR7—7F 21
  (Chorley)
Sandringham Rd. PR7—1E 22
  (Eccleston)
Sandsdale Av. PR2—6C 4
Sandwick Clo. PR2—6K 3
Sandybrook Clo. PR2—6E 4
Sandy Croft. PR2—2F 9
Sandyforth La. PR4—4E 2
Sandygate La. PR3—1F 3
Sandy La. PR4—3B 2
Sandy La. PR5—6J 15
Sandy La. PR6—3G 17
Sandy Pl. PR5—6J 15
Saul St. PR1—4K 7
Saunders Clo. PR4—3B 10
Saunders La. PR4—4C 10
Savick Av. PR2—3B 6
Savick Clo. PR5—5F 13
Savick Rd. PR2—7H 3
Savick Way. PR2—1C 6
Saville St. PR7—3G 25
Savoy St. PR1—5J 7
Sawley Cres. PR2—2F 9
Saxon Hey. PR2—1G 7
Scarlet St. PR6—1J 25
Scawfell Rd. PR7—3F 25
Schleswig St. PR1—4A 8
Schleswig Way. PR5—6E 14
School Field. PR5—1F 17
School La. PR5—5C 14
School La. PR5—3E 12
  (Bamber Bridge)
School La. PR5—5K 11
  (Farington)
School La. PR5—4H 15
  (Leyland)
School La. PR6—7F 17
School La. PR7—4B 20
School St. PR1—5J 7
School St. PR5—2F 13
  (Bamber Bridge)
School St. PR5—4K 15
  (Leyland)
Scotforth Rd. PR1—4C 8
Scott's Wood. PR2—4H 3
Sedberg St. PR2—1H 7
Sedgwick St. PR1—3A 8
Seedlee Rd. PR5—7G 13
Seed St. PR1—4K 7
Sefton Rd. PR5—2D 12
Selborne St. PR1—6A to 5B 8
Selby St. PR1—3H 7
Selkirk Dri. PR5—3D 12
Sellers St. PR1—3C 8
Sephton St. PR5—5A 12
Sergeant St. PR5—5F 13

Seven Acres. PR5—1G 17
Sevenoaks. PR7—4G 25
Seven Stars Rd. PR5—7F 15
Severn Dri. PR5—3D 12
Severn Hill. PR2—3G 3
Seymour Rd. PR2—1G 7
Seymour St. PR6—1H 25
Shade La. PR7—6H 25
Shady La. PR5—1B 16
Shaftesbury Av. PR1—6F 7
Shaftesbury Av. PR4—5D 10
Shaftesbury Pl. PR7—7F 21
Shakespeare Rd. PR1—3D 8
(in two parts)
Shakespeare Ter. PR6—5H 21
Shalgrove Field. PR2—4G 3
Sharoe Grn. La. PR2—4J 3
Sharoe Grn. La. S. PR2—7A 4
Sharoe Grn. Pk. PR2—6A 4
Sharoe Mt. Av. PR2—4K 3
Sharratts Path. PR7—4D 24
Shawbrook Clo. PR7—2A 20
Shaw Brook Rd. PR5—1F 19
Shaw Brow. PR6—7F 17
Shaw Hill. PR6—1F 21
Shaw Hill Dri. PR6—1F 21
Shaw Hill St. PR7—1G 25
Shaw St. PR1—3A 8
Sheep Hill La. PR4—6D 10
Sheep Hill La. PR6
—4D 16 to 3F 17
Sheffield Dri. PR2—2B 6
Sheldon Ct. PR1—3K 7
(off Moor La.)
Shelley Clo. PR7—7D 24
Shelley Dri. PR7—3F 23
Shelley Rd. PR2—2G to 3H 7
Shepherd St. PR1—5A 8
Sherbourne Cres. PR1—1B 8
Sherbourne St. PR6—1H 25
Sherburn Rd. PR1—2J 11
Sherdley Rd. PR6—6B 12
Sherwood Pl. PR6—7H 21
Sherwood Way. PR2—5A 4
Shire Bank Cres. PR2—6J 3
Shop La. PR5—1H 13
Shuttle St. PR1—4B 8
Shuttleworth Rd. PR1—2K 7
Shuttling Fields La. PR5
—4G to 3J 13
Sibbering Brow. PR7—7A 20
Sidgreaves La. PR4—6A 2
Silsden Av. PR6—6D 4
Silverdale Clo. PR5—1K 19
Silverdale Dri. PR2—6D 4
Silverdale Rd. PR6—1J 25
Silvester Rd. PR7—2G 25
Simmons Av. PR5—3B 12
Simpson St. PR1—4K 7
Singleton Clo. PR2—4K 3
Singleton Row. PR1—3K 7
Singleton Way. PR2—4K 3
Sion Clo. PR2—7F 5
Sion Hill. PR2—7F 5
Six Acre La. PR4—7A 10
Sizehouse St. PR1—4K 7
Sizer St. PR1—3K 7
Skeffington Rd. PR1—2B 8
Skip La. PR4—2A 10
Skipton Cres. PR2—6E 4
Slade St. PR1—5J 7
Slaidburn Pl. PR2—2G 9
Slaidburn Rd. PR2—2F 9
Slater La. PR5—6C 14 to 6F 15
Smalley Croft. PR1—2K 11
Smith Clo. PR2—2J 5
Smith Croft. PR5—6D 14
Smithhill's Clo. PR6—6J 21
Smith St. PR5—5F 13
Smith St. PR6—6G 17
Smith St. PR7—2H 25
Smithy Brow. WN6—7E 22
Smithy Clo. PR6—1K 17
Smithy La. PR6—1K 17

Smithy St. PR5—5E 12
Snipewood. PR7—2D 22
Snow Hill. PR1—4K 7
Sod Hall La. PR4 & PR5—1C 14
Sod Hall Rd. PR4—7E 10
Sollam's Clo. PR5—3F 13
Solway Clo. PR1—2J 11
Somerset Av. PR7—6G 21
Somerset Pk. PR2—4F 3
Somerset Rd. PR1—3A 8
Somerset Rd. PR5—4K 15
Sorrel Ct. PR1—3G 11
South Av. PR6—4D 10
South Av. PR7—2H 25
Southbrook Rd. PR5—5H 15
S. Cliff St. PR1—6J 7
Southdowns Rd. PR7—2H 25
South Dri. PR2—4J 3
South End. PR1—7J 7
Southern Av. PR1—6C 8
Southern Pde. PR1—6B 8
Southey Clo. PR2—4K 3
Southfield Dri. PR4—6D 10
Southgate. PR1—3K 7
Southgate. PR2—6H 3
Southgates. PR7—5B 24
South Gro. PR2—3J 3
Southlands Av. PR5—4C 12
Southlands Dri. PR5—7D 14
S. Meadow La. PR1—6J 7
S. Meadow St. PR1—4A 8
Southport Rd. PR5 & PR7
—5B 18
Southport Rd. PR7—6D 20
Southport Ter. PR6—1J 25
S. Ribble St. PR5—6D 8
South Rd. PR7—7C 24
Southside. PR7—4A 20
South Ter. PR7—3B 20
South View. PR5—6B 12
(off School La.)
South View. PR5—6A 12
(off Watkin La.)
S. View Ter. PR5—6J 15
Spa Rd. PR1—4H 7
Spa St. PR1—4H 7
Spendmore La. PR7—7B 24
Spey Clo. PR5—6G 15
Spinners Sq. PR5—6E 12
Spinney Brow. PR2—7D 4
Spinney Clo. PR4—5D 10
Spinney Clo. PR6—1F 21
Spinney, The. PR1—2D 10
Spinney, The. PR6—4G 21
Spring Bank. PR1—5J 7
Springcroft. PR5—3A 16
Springfield Rd. PR5—7F 15
Springfield Rd. PR7—7G 21
(Chorley)
Springfield Rd. PR7—7C 24
(Coppull)
Springfield Rd. N. PR7—7C 24
Springfield St. PR1—3J 7
Spring Gdns. PR1—3K 11
Spring Gdns. PR5—6H 15
Spring Meadow. PR5—5C 16
Springs Cres. PR6—2J 21
Springs Rd. PR6—5H 21
(in two parts)
Spring St. PR5—5K 15
Springwood Dri. PR7—3J 25
Square, The. PR5—4K 15
(Leyland)
Square, The. PR5—7F 9
(Walton-le-Dale)
Squires Ga. Rd. PR2—1G 7
Squires Rd. PR1—6G 7
Squirrel Fold. PR2—2F 9
Squirrel's Chase. PR5—6A 12
Stackcroft. PR6—4E 16
Stafford Rd. PR1—3A 8
Staining Av. PR2—3D 6
Standish St. PR7—1H 25
Stanhope St. PR1—2H 7
Stanifield Clo. PR5—3K 15

Stanifield La. PR5—4K 15
Stanley Av. PR1—7J 7
Stanley Av. PR4—3B 10
Stanley Av. PR5—2A 16
Stanley Croft. PR4—1F 3
Stanleyfield Rd. PR1—3A 8
Stanley Gro. PR1—1E 10
Stanley Pl. PR1—5J 7
Stanley Pl. PR7—7G 21
Stanley Rd. PR5—2A 16
Stanley St. PR1—4B 8
Stanley St. PR5—5K 15
Stanley St. PR6—1J 25
Stanley Ter. PR1—5J 7
Stanning St. PR5—6J 15
Stansted Rd. PR7—1E 24
Starkie St. PR1—5K 7
Starkie St. PR5—5K 15
Starrgate Dri. PR2—3C 6
Station Brow. PR5—6K 15
Station Rd. PR4—5D 10
Station Rd. PR5—3E to 6E 12
(Bamber Bridge)
Station Rd. PR5—3C 14
(Hesketh Bank)
Station Rd. PR7—7D 24
Staveley Pl. PR2—2C 6
Steeley La. PR6—1H 25
Steeple View. PR2—4H 7
Stefano Rd. PR1—4C 8
Stephendale Av. PR5—5H 13
Stephenson St. PR6—1J 25
Stevenson Av. PR5—3A 16
Stewart St. PR1—4H 7
Stiles Av. PR4—4A 10
Stirling Clo. PR5—5A 16
Stirling Clo. PR6—1J 25
Stockdale Cres. PR5—6F 13
Stocks La. PR7—5G 23
Stocks Rd. PR2—2G to 3G 7
Stocks St. PR1—4J 7
Stonebridge Clo. PR5—5C 12
Stone Croft. PR1—3H 11
Stonecroft Rd. PR5—7F 15
Stonefield. PR1—1J 11
Stonefold Av. PR4—4A 10
Stonehouse Grn. PR6—3F 17
Stoney Butts. PR2—4B 6
Stoneygate. PR1—5A 8
Stoney Holt. PR5—5C 16
Stoney La. PR5—7C 12
Stony Bank. PR6—1K 17
Stonyhurst Av. PR2—4G 25
Stour Lodge. PR2—5G 3
Strand Rd. PR1—5H 7
Strand St. W. PR2—4G 7
Stratford Dri. PR2—7H 3
Stratford Rd. PR6—7H 21
Strathmore Gro. PR7—1E 25
Strathmore Rd. PR2—7J 3
Stricklands La. PR1—1H 11
Strutt St. PR1—3B 8
Stryands. PR4—4A 10
Stuart Clo. PR2—1E 8
Stuart Rd. PR2—1E 8
Studfold. PR7—5F 21
Studholme Av. PR1—3J 11
Studholme Clo. PR1—3J 11
Studholme Cres. PR1—3J 11
Stump La. PR7 & PR6—7H 21
Sturminster Clo. PR1—3J 11
Suffolk Clo. PR5—1G 19
Suffolk Rd. PR1—3A 8
Sulby Dri PR2—6F 5
Sulby Gro. PR2—6G 5
Summer Trees Av. PR2—1B 6
Sumner St. PR5—5J 15
Sumpter Croft. PR1—5C 8
Sunbury Av. PR1—2H 11
Sunningdale. PR4—1F 3
Sunny Brow. PR7—6E 24
Surgeon's Ct. PR1—5K 7
Surrey St. PR1—3A 8
Sussex St. PR1—3A 8
(in two parts)

Sutcliffe St. PR7—1H 25
Sutton Dri. PR2—4B 6
Sutton Gro. PR6—3K 21
Swallow Av. PR1—1J 11
Swansea St. PR2—4G 7
Swansey La. PR5—5G 17
Swan St. PR1—4C 8
Swarbrick St. PR1—4A 8
Swill Brook La. PR1—6C 8
Sycamore Av. PR7—4B 20
Sycamore Clo. PR2—5C 4
Sycamore Ct. PR7—3F 25
Sycamore Dri. PR1—2J 11
Sycamore Rd. PR2—2E 8
Sycamore Rd. PR6—5H 21
Syd Brook La. PR5 & L40
—7A 18
Syke Hill. PR1—5A 8
Syke St. PR1—5A 8
Sylvancroft. PR2—6E 2
Sylvan Gro. PR5—3G 13
Symonds Rd. PR2—1J 7

Tabley La. PR4—2B 2
Tag Croft. PR2—6D 2
Tag Farm Ct. PR2—6D 2
Tag La. PR4 & PR2—5D 2 to 7F 3
Talbot Dri. PR5—5B 20
Talbot Rd. PR1—7J 7
(Penwortham)
Talbot Rd. PR1—5H 7
(Preston)
Talbot Rd. PR5—4G 15
Talbot Row. PR7—6B 20
Talbot St. PR1—1H 7
Talbot St. PR2—1H 7
Talbot St. PR6—6J 21
Tamar Clo. PR5—7K 15
Tamar St. PR1—4E 8
Tanhouse La. PR6—1K 21
Tannersmith La. L40—3B 22
Tansley Av. PR7—7B 24
Tanterton Hall Rd. PR2—5D 2
Tanyard Clo. PR7—7B 24
Tarn Clo. PR1—1D 10
Tarn Hows Clo. PR7—3F 25
Tatton St. PR6—1H 25
Taunton St. PR1—3D 8
Taylor St. PR1—6H 7
Taylor St. PR7—3F 25
Tay St. PR1—6H 7
Tees St. PR1—2C 8
Temperance St. PR6—7J 21
Tenby Rd. PR1—6A 8
Tennyson Av. PR2—2E 8
Tennyson Pl. PR5—3D 12
Tennyson Rd. PR1—3D 8
(in three parts)
Tenterfield St. PR1—4K 7
Terrace St. PR1—3C 8
Teven St. PR5—4E 12
Theatre St. PR1—5K 7
Thirlmere Rd. PR1—3F 9
Thirlmere Rd. PR2—2E 24
Thistlecroft. PR2—6E 2
Thistleton Rd. PR2—4C 6
Thomas St. PR1—5C 8
Thompson St. PR1—3D 8
Thornfield Av. PR1—1F 9
Thorngate. PR1—1F 11
Thorngate Clo. PR1—1F 11
Thornhill Rd. PR5—6F 15
Thornhill Rd. PR6—5J 21
Thornley Pl. PR2—1G 9
Thornley Rd. PR2—1G 9
Thornpark Dri. PR2—4B 6
Thorn St. PR1—2C 8
Thornton Av. PR2—7F 3
Thornton Dri. PR5—2K 13
(Coup Green)
Thornton Dri. PR5—2G 15
(Farington Moss)
Thorntrees Av. PR2—3B 6
Thorpe Clo. PR1—3K 7
Threefields. PR2—6E 2

Three Nooks. PR5—1G 17
Threlfall St. PR2—3G 7
Thropps La. PR4—6A 10
Thurnham Rd. PR2—4C 6
Thurston Rd. PR5—5J 15
Tiber St. PR1—5B 8
Timber Brook. PR7—5E 20
Tincklers La. L40 & PR7
—3B & 2C 22
Tinkerfield. PR2—4J 3
Tinkler's Rd. PR6—2K 25
Tinniswood. PR2—3F 7
Tintern Av. PR7—3H 25
Titan Way. PR5—4D 14
Tithe Barn La. PR5 & PR7
—2H 19
Tithebarn St. PR1—4A 8
(in three parts)
Tiverton Clo. PR2—3K 3
Todd La. N. PR5—2C 12
Todd La. S. PR5—5C 12
Tollgate. PR1—1J 11
Tolsey Dri. PR4—3B 10
Tom Benson Way. PR2—6D 2
Tomlinson Rd. PR2—2G 7
Tomlinson Rd. PR5—4H 15
Tootell St. PR7—2F 25
Top Acre. PR4—4A 10
Top o'th'Lane. PR6—3J 17
Tower Grn. PR2—4K 3
Tower La. PR2—4K 3
Town Brow. PR5—4D 16
Towngate. PR5—6J 15
Towngate. PR7—7D 18
Towngate Ct. PR7—1D 22
Town La. PR6—7G 17
Town La. PR7—7K 23
(Coppull)
Town La. PR7—7E 22
(Heskin Green)
Townley La. PR1—1A 10
Townley St. PR6—1H 25
Townsway. PR5—5C 12
Trafalgar Clo. PR2—1H 7
Trafalgar St. PR7—6H 21
Trafford St. PR1—2J 7
Tramway La. PR5—7H 13
Travers St. PR2—4G 7
Trawden Cres. PR2—7E 4
Triangle, The. PR2—7J 3
Trinity Fold. PR1—4K 7
Trinity Pl. PR1—4K 7
Trinity Rd. PR7—1F 25
Troon Ct. PR1—6E 6
Troutbeck Pl. PR2—6E 4
Troutbeck Rd. PR7—3F 25
Trout St. PR1—5C 8
Trower St. PR1—6B 8
Truro Ct. PR1—3D 8
Truro Pl. PR1—3D 8
Tudor Av. PR1—4F 9
Tudor Av. PR2—2A 6
Tudor Clo. PR2—3B 6
Tudor Croft. PR5—6C 12
Tuer St. PR5—4H 15
Tulketh Av. PR2—3F 7
Tulketh Brow. PR2—2G 7
Tulketh Cres. PR2—3G 7
(in two parts)
Tulketh Rd. PR2—3F 7
Tunbridge Pl. PR1—3D 8
Tunbridge St. PR1—3D 8
Tunbrook Av. PR2—2K 5
Tunley Holme. PR5—1F 17
Turbary, The. PR2—1G 7
Turks Head Yd. PR1—5A 8
Turner Av. PR5—6A 12
Turner St. PR1—3A 8
Turnfield. PR2—5D 2
Turnpike, The. PR5—5H 3
Turpin Grn. La. PR5—5K 15
Turton Dri. PR6—6J 21
Tuson Dri. PR2—4J 7
Tuson Ho. PR1—3J 11
Tweed St. PR1—4H 7

Tyndale Clo. PR5—1K 19
Tyne St. PR1—6H 7
Tyne St. PR5—4F 13

Ullswater Rd. PR2—7C 4
Ullswater Rd. PR7—2F 25
Ulnes Walton La. PR5—3B 18
Underwood. PR2—1G 7
Union St. PR1—4K 7
Union St. PR6—6G 17
Union St. PR7—7G 21

Vale, The. PR2—6K 3
Valley Rd. PR1—7G 7
Valley View. PR2—7A 4
Valley View. PR5—2A 12
Valley View. PR6—1J 25
Varley St. PR1—2A 8
Ventnor Pl. PR2—7E 2
Ventnor Rd. PR7—2F 25
Vernon St. PR1—3K 7
Vevey St. PR5—5J 15
Vicarage Clo. PR2—7K 3
Vicarage Clo. PR7—4B 20
Vicarage La. PR2—7K 3
Vicarage La. PR5—3K & 4K 9
Vicarage St. PR6—6H 21
Vicarsfields Rd. PR5—7J 15
Victoria Ct. PR2—1J 7
Victoria Mans. PR2—4E 6
Victoria Pde. PR2—3F 7
Victoria Pk. Av. PR2—3B 6
Victoria Pk. Dri. PR2—3B 6
Victoria Quay. PR2—5E 6
Victoria Rd. PR2—1K 7
Victoria Rd. PR5—6C 8
Victoria St. PR1—3J 7
Victoria St. PR5—5B 12
Victoria St. PR6—7K 17
Victoria St. PR7—1H 25
Victoria Ter. PR5—6J 15
Victoria Ter. PR6—6H 21
View St. PR7—1E 22
Village Croft. PR7—4B 20
Village Dri. PR2—2F 9
Village Grn. La. PR2—5D 2
Villiers St. PR1—2J 7
Villiers St. PR1—2J 7
Vinery, The. PR4—5D 10
Vine St. PR1—4H 7
Vine St. PR7—6G 21

Waddington Rd. PR2—2G 9
Wade Brook Rd. PR5—1B 18
Wadham Rd. PR1—6B 8
Waingate. PR2—2J 5
Waingate Ct. PR2—2J 5
Waldon St. PR1—3E 8
Walgarth Dri. PR7—1E 24
Walkdale. PR4—3B 10
Walker Pl. PR1—5B 8
Walker's La. PR2—4F 3
Walker St. PR1—4K 7
Walled Garden, The. PR6
—1F 21
Walletts Rd. PR7—2F 25
Walnut Clo. PR1—2F 11
Walton Av. PR1—2F 11
Walton Grn. PR5—1D 12
Walton's Pde. PR1—5J 7
Walton Summit Ind. Est. PR5
—6H 13
Walton Summit Rd. PR5—7G 13
Walton View. PR1—4D 8
Wanstead St. PR1—4E 8
Warbrick Av. PR2—3A 6
Warbury St. PR1—3E 8
Ward's End. PR1—5A 8
Wards New Row. PR5—6B 12
Ward St. PR5—6B 12
Ward St. PR6—1J 25
Warings, The. PR7—4G 23

Warner Rd. PR1—3D 8
Warton Pl. PR7—7E 20
Warton St. PR1—6H 7
Warwick Clo. PR2—7J 3
Warwick Rd. PR5—7G 15
(Leyland)
Warwick Rd. PR5—1D 12
(Walton-le-Dale)
Warwick Rd. PR7—1E 22
Warwick St. PR1—4K 7
Wasdale Clo. PR5—1K 19
Washington La. PR7—5C 20
Waterford Clo. PR2—6C 4
Water Head. PR2—1F 7
Watering Pool La. PR5—3B 12
Water La. PR2—4G & 3H 7
(in two parts)
Waterloo Rd. PR2—2F 7
Waterloo St. PR7—6H 21
Waterloo Ter. PR2—3G 7
Water St. PR5—3E 12
Water St. PR6—1K 17
Water St. PR7—7G 21
Watery La. PR1—6C & 4D 8
(in two parts)
Watery La. PR2—4F 7
Watkin La. PR5—5A 12
Watkin Rd. PR6—6F 17
Watling St. Rd. PR2
—7K 3 to 6F 5
Waverley Dri. PR4—6D 10
Waverley Gdns. PR2—2E 8
Waverley Rd. PR1—3D 8
Webster St. PR2—3G 7
Weeton Pl. PR2—3C 6
Weld Av. PR7—3G 25
Weldbank La. PR7—3G 25
Weldbank St. PR7—3G 25
Welfield Rd. PR1—4H 7
Wellfield Av. PR5—5H 15
Wellfield Rd. PR5—6A 12
Wellington Av. PR5—6K 15
Wellington Pl. PR5—3D 12
Wellington Rd. PR2—3F 7
Wellington St. PR1—4H 7
Wellington St. PR7—6G 21
Well Orchard. PR5—1F 17
Wells St. PR1—4D 8
Welsby Rd. PR5—6F 15
Wembley Av. PR1—7F 7
Wensley Pl. PR2—7D 4
Wentworth Clo. PR1—6E 6
Wentworth Dri. PR3—1G 3
Werneth Clo. PR1—4K 11
Wesley St. PR5—5F 13
West Av. PR2—5E 2
West Bank. PR7—7G 21
Westbourne Rd. PR7—2F 25
Westbrook Cres. PR2—1E 6
Westby Pl. PR2—3D 6
West Cliff. PR1—6J 7
W. Cliff Ter. PR1—6J 7
(in two parts)
West Cres. PR6—1G 3
West Dri. PR5—3B 16
West End. PR1—6E 6
Westend Av. PR7—7B 24
Westerlong. PR2—3B 6
Western Dri. PR5—5F 15
Westfield. PR5—5A 12
Westfield Dri. PR2—2E 8
Westfield Dri. PR5—4K 13
(Gregson Lane)
Westfield Dri. PR5—5F 15
(Leyland)
Westgate. PR2—6H 3
Westgate. PR5—6H 15
Westhoughton Rd. PR7—7K 25
Westlands. PR5—7E 14
Westleigh Rd. PR2—3D 6
West Meadow. PR2—1C 6
Westminster Pl. PR7—7C 18
Westminster Rd. PR7—1G 25
Westmorland Clo. PR1—1F 11
Westmorland Clo. PR5—7G 15

Weston St. PR2—4H 7
W. Paddock. PR5—6G 15
W. Park Av. PR2—2C 6
W. Park La. PR2—2E 6
West Rd. PR2—1K 7
West Strand. PR4—1G 7
West St. PR7—1G 25
West Ter. PR7—3B 20
West View. PR1—2C 8
West View. PR5—6E 12
W. View Ter. PR1—4G 7
Westway. PR2—7A 4
West Way. PR7—6D 20
Westway Ct. PR2—7A 4
Westwell Rd. PR6—6H 21
Westwood Rd. PR5—2G 17
(Clayton Green)
Westwood Rd. PR5—4J 15
(Leyland)
Wetherall St. PR2—3H 7
Whalley Rd. PR7—4F 23
Whalley St. PR5—3F 13
Whalley St. PR7—1G 25
Wham Hey. PR4—6E 10
Wham La. PR4—6E 10
Wharfedale Av. PR2—6E 4
Wharfedale Rd. PR5—7J 15
Wheatfield. PR5—6C 14
Wheelton La. PR5—4J 15
Whernside Cres. PR2—6D 4
Whernside Way. PR5—5A 16
Whinfield Av. PR6—6H 21
Whinfield La. PR2—4D 6
Whinfield Pl. PR2—4D 6
Whinnyfield La. PR4—1A 2
Whinny La. PR7—3C 20
Whitby Av. PR2—6D 2
Whitby Pl. PR2—6D 2
Whitefield Rd. PR1—1E 10
Whitefield Rd. E. PR1—1E 10
Whitefield Rd. W. PR1—1E 10
Whitefriar Clo. PR2—6E 2
Whitegate Fold. PR7—5C 24
Whiteholme Pl. PR2—3C 6
Whitelens Av. PR2—3A 6
White Meadow. PR2—1C 6
Whitendale Dri. PR5—5F 13
Whitethorn Clo. PR6—4E 16
Whitethorn Sq. PR2—3B 6
Whitewell Rd. PR2—1G 9
Whitmore Clo. PR2—2G 9
Whitmore Gro. PR2—2G 9
Whitmore Pl. PR2—2G 9
Whittam Rd. PR7—3F 25
Whittingham La. PR2—1H 5
Whittingham La. PR3—1H 3
Whittle Brow. PR7—7A 24
Whittle Hill. PR4—1C 2
Whitworth Dri. PR7—1E 24
Wholesome La. PR4—7C 10
Wigan La. PR7—7H 25
Wigan Rd. PR5 & PR7
—6E 12 to 6B 20
Wignall St. PR1—3C 8
Wigton Av. PR5—7F 15
Wilbraham St. PR1—3C 8
Wilderwood Clo. PR6—4G 17
Wildman St. PR1—2J 7
Wilkinson St. PR5—5B 12
William Henry St. PR1—4C 8
William St. PR7—2J 7
Willow Clo. PR1—1E 10
Willow Clo. PR5—4K 13
(Gregson Lane)
Willow Clo. PR5—5A 12
(Lostock Hall)
Willow Coppice. PR2—1C 6
Willow Cres. PR2—2D 8
Willow Dri. PR7—5B 24
Willowfield. PR6—3G 17
Willow Rd. PR5—1B 18
Willow Rd. PR6—5J 21
Willows, The. PR7—7C 24
Willow Tree Av. PR3—1H 3
Willow Tree Cres. PR5—5F 15

Willow Way. PR4—6D 10
Wilmar Rd. PR5—4A 16
Wilmot Rd. PR2—1E 8
Wilson Cres. PR5—3B 16
Wilton Gro. PR1—1E 10
Winchester Av. PR7—5J 25
Winckley Gdns. PR1—5K 7
Winckley Rd. PR1—6H 7
Winckley Sq. PR1—5K 7
Winckley St. PR1—5K 7
Windermere Av. PR5—3J 15
Windermere Rd. PR1—3G 9
Windermere Rd. PR2—7C 4
Windermere Rd. PR6—1J 25
Windsor Av. PR1—2G 11
Windsor Av. PR2—2F 7
Windsor Av. PR4—4E 10
Windsor Clo. PR7—1F 25
Windsor Dri. PR2—5H 3
Windsor Rd. PR5—2D 12
Windsor Rd. PR7—1F 25
  (Chorley)
Windsor Rd. PR7—1E 22
  (Eccleston)
Winery La. PR5—7C 8
Wingates. PR1—2G 11
Winmarleigh Rd. PR2—3F 7
Winslow Clo. PR1—3J 11
Winsor Av. PR5—6K 15
Winster Clo. PR5—1K 13
Winton Av. PR2—5K 3
Withington La. PR7—6G 23
Withnel Gro. PR6—6J 21
Withy Gro. Clo. PR5—4F 13
Withy Gro. Cres. PR5—4F 13
Withy Gro. Rd. PR5—4F 13
Withy Pde. PR2—7J 3

Withy Trees Av. PR5—5F 13
Withy Trees Clo. PR5—4F 13
Witton St. PR1—4B 8
Wolseley Pl. PR1—5A 8
Wolseley Rd. PR1—7J 7
Woodacre Rd. PR2—2G 9
Woodale Rd. PR6—2F 17
Wood Bank. PR1—2G 11
Woodcock Est. PR5—7B 12
Woodcock Fold. PR7—1E 22
Woodcock La. PR7—4G 23
Woodcroft Clo. PR1—3G 11
Wood End Rd. PR6—3E 16
Woodfall. PR7—6F 21
Woodfield. PR5—7J 13
Woodfield Rd. PR7—6G 21
Woodford Copse. PR7—1D 24
Wood Grn. PR5—4G 15
Woodhart La. PR7—3E 22
Woodhouse Gro. PR1—5H 7
Woodland Grange. PR1—2H 11
Woodland Gro. PR1—7F 7
Woodlands Av. PR1—2H 11
Woodlands Av. PR2—2E 8
Woodlands Av. PR5—3G 13
Woodlands Dri. PR2—3J 3
Woodlands Dri. PR5—5H 15
Woodlands Gro. PR2—2K 5
Woodlands Meadow. PR7
                    —5G 25
Wood La. L40—3A 22
Wood La. PR7 & WN6
                —4F to 7G 23
Woodlea Rd. PR5—6H 15
Woodmancote. PR7—5F 21
Woodplumpton La. PR3—1G 3

Woodplumpton Rd. PR2—1F 7
Woods Grn. PR1—6J 7
Woodside. PR5—2A 16
Woodside. PR7—4J 25
  (Chorley)
Woodside. PR7—4A 20
  (Euxton)
Woodside Av. PR2—7J 3
  (Fulwood)
Woodside Av. PR2—1E 8
  (Ribbleton)
Woodside Av. PR4—6D 10
Woodside Av. PR6—5F 17
Woodstock Clo. PR5—5C 12
Woodville Rd. PR1—3H 11
Woodville Rd. PR6—7K 25
Woodville Rd. PR7—7G 21
Woodville Rd. W. PR1—3G 11
Woodville St. PR5—3K 15
Woodway. PR2—7G 3
Wookey Clo. PR2—5D 4
Worcester Av. PR5—6K 15
Worcester Pl. PR7—5J 25
Worden Clo. PR5—7H 15
Worden La. PR5—7J 15
Worden Rd. PR2—1H 7
Wordsworth Pl. PR5—3D 12
Wordsworth Ter. PR6—5H 21
Worthing Rd. PR2—7E 2
Worthy St. PR6—1J 25
Wray Cres. PR5—1B 18
Wren Av. PR1—7J 7
Wrennalls La. PR7—3D 22
Wren St. PR1—3B 8
Wrights Fold. PR5—6A 16
Wright St. PR6—7J 21

Wychnor. PR2—4F 3
Wymundsley. PR7—5E 20
Wyresdale Cres. PR2—7D 4
Wyresdale Dri. PR5—7K 15
Wyre St. PR2—3G 7

Yarrow Ga. PR7—2J 25
Yarrow Pl. PR5—6F 15
Yarrow Rd. PR5—6F 15
Yarrow Rd. PR6—2J 25
Yates St. PR7—2F 25
Yeadon Gro. PR7—1E 24
Yeovil Ct. PR1—3D 8
Yewland Av. PR7—5H 23
Yewlands Av. PR2—5J 3
Yewlands Av. PR5—4F 13
  (Bamber Bridge)
Yewlands Av. PR5—5H 15
  (Leyland)
Yewlands Cres. PR2—5J 3
Yewlands Dri. PR2—5J 3
Yewlands Dri. PR5—5H 15
Yew Tree Av. PR2—1J 5
Yew Tree Av. PR7—3A 20
Yew Trees Av. PR2—7G 5
York Av. PR2—7J 3
York Clo. PR5—7G 15
  (Leyland)
York Clo. PR5—2D 12
  (Walton-le-Dale)
York St. PR7—1H 25
Young Av. PR5—5A 16

Zetland St. PR1—5C 8